Timeless Writings 32

Tatay Jobo Elizes
Feb. 2017

Published by Tatay Jobo Elizes, Self-Publisher

This book is published and printed under the benevolent consent and attribution (borrowed) from various authors/heirs/associates compiled for this purpose of making their articles and essays available to the public and promote reading and writing among Filipinos, young and old. Authors own the copyrights to their writings. Owners can withdraw or rescind their consent anytime and will be edited out in next printing. Printing of this book is using the present day method of Print-On-Demand (POD) or Book-On-Demand (BOD) systems, where prints will never run out of copies. Owners are free to republish or reprint with other publishers and printers anytime. This book is dedicated to all Filipinos.

ISBN Codes

ISBN – 13: 978 – 1542898331   and
ISBN – 10: 1542898331

Self-Publisher's Details:
Contact: job_elizes@yahoo.com
Websites: http:tinyurl.com/mj76ccq +
www.jobelizes6.wix.com/mysite

Contents

Includes Lichauco-Ramos Letters, etc.   **4**

1.

Publisher's Note on the Lichauco-Ramos Open Letters

Dateline, 1991
Originally published by Citizens Committee on the National Crisis
Printed by Claretian Publications and open to the public

The Citizens Committee on the National Crisis (CCNC) is pleased to make available to the public in convenient form the exchange of open letters between political economist Alejandro Lichauco and Defense Secretary Fidel V. Ramos on the economic crisis. In the view of the CCNC, these open letters are of historic significance for the light they cast not only on the nature of the crisis but, more importantly, on the reasons behind it.

The exchange, which began with Lichauco's letter to Ramos under date of December 8,1990, was serialized in NEWSDAY. BULLETIN started serializing Lichauco's letter, but after the third installment the serialization was abruptly terminated without as much as an explanation from the editors. That incident was one of the factors which prompted the CCNC to have Lichauco's letters printed along with the exchange that followed.

To our knowledge, Lichauco's letter is the first to have presented an organized and documented explanation for the crisis which departs radically from the usual version of it. The crisis has been habitually explained in terms of graft and corruption. Lichauco demolishes this theory of the crisis. He attributes the crisis to what he describes as the treason of policy" Treason, not necessarily as the crime is defined in the penal code, but in its realistic economic sense.

Lichauco's thesis touches a responsive chord. Treason

is an explosive term, not to be used lightly in a debate of public issues, but it is a term now being used with frequency, and in no less than the halls of Congress. Only recently, the Majority Floor Leader of the Senate, Senator Teofisto Guingona, and the populist Senator Joseph Estrada, charged the nation's debt negotiators with economic treason. Senators Pimentel, Estrada and Romulo have filed a bill that would outlaw the practice of the nation's debt negotiators in accepting positions with the IMFAVB on the ground that such a practice opens up possibilities of treason.

In what sense the nation's vital policies constitute treason Lichauco explains with meticulous logic, and in that we believe lies the signal contribution of his open letter to the nations politicalization.

In reprinting the exchange of letters between Lichauco and the Defense Secretary, the CCNC has embarked on its first public interest project. We are a non-formal study group increasingly disturbed by the trend of national affairs, and convinced that elections are not a solution to the country's predicament. In fact, we are convinced that elections can only aggravate that predicament. The reason for this is that we suffer from a political system that by its very structure and processes is anti-democratic and productive of policies that are essentially treasonous in character. Who can believe we have a democracy when by and large only multimillionaires can get elected to Congress and the Presidency? How many of our Congressmen and Senators are in the payroll of vested local and foreign interests? Until and unless the structure of the political system is overhauled, there can be no real democracy in this country, and the treason of which Lichauco speaks can only persist.

We believe that citizens and organizations genuinely concerned with the state of the nation should work for the suspension of elections scheduled next year and for the immediate reorganization of Government under a multisectoral body that would forge a blueprint for the nation based on independence, democratization, development and social justice. For one, we cannot keep on the way we are if we are to catch up with our Asian neighbors, economically and militarily.

The nation cannot afford another election under the

existing political system. That system must first be changed before elections are held.

In the meanwhile, we urge media to give the widest possible exposure to the materials contained in this pamphlet. It is time that the nation confronted the explosive issue raised by the Lichauco-Ramos exchange.

ooo0ooo

2.

An Open Letter to Secretary Fidel V. Ramos on the Economic Crisis and the Treason of Policy

by Alejandro Lichauco

Hon. Fidel V. Ramos
Secretary
Department of National Defense
Camp Aguinaldo
Quezon City

Dear Secretary Ramos:

Early last month media reported on the views you expressed during the inauguration of Camp Narciso R. Ramos in Tayug, Pangasinan, and you were quoted, concerning the economic crisis, to have said that it is "the product principally of a dwindling foreign exchange." **(Philippines Journal, Nov. 12).**

I am writing this open letter not only because I disagree with your interpretation of a malady which, in your own words, "affects everybody," but mainly because I feel that the people who follow your pronouncements, and they must be substantial considering the high regard with which you are generally held, should be disabused of the notion that ours is a simple crisis of foreign exchange. Your interpretation, with due respect, reinforces the position of economic functionaries who, all these years, have misled our people into thinking that the economic problem is essentially a balance of payments problems that justifies the orgy of foreign borrowing in which they have indulged.

If the crisis is due primarily to a shortage of dollars, then the remedy obviously lies in replenishing our dollar reserves at all cost, even if that would mean borrowing under any conditions that our creditors might impose. That, in fact, is what our economic managers have done and the result has been absolute disaster.

I agree with you that "the threat against peace and order today is not so much from military or communist rebels" as it is from the economic crisis. But precisely because the crisis constitutes the greatest threat to peace and order, as you correctly perceived, it becomes all the more necessary, and urgent, that it be diagnosed correctly so that it may be approached properly and effectively. Otherwise, that crisis can only aggravate, which is what is happening. And we don't have much time, Mr. Secretary, to forge a national consensus on the real nature of the crisis and on how it should be approached.

If we are to come to grips with the crisis, the first step obviously is to recognize its real nature and the root factors that have given it rise. A dwindling foreign exchange is merely one of the many aspects of the crisis and is far from its cause, much less its main cause. The crisis stems from a more fundamental and malevolent disorder, which should be of particular interest to your department as the agency of government most concerned with national security.

This letter will inescapably be lengthy because it will trace the origins of our crisis, and establish the basis for the possible finding by your department of sabotage and economic treason. The nature of the crisis and the real factors behind it.

The essence of our crisis lies in the fact that, heavily in debt and short of dollars, we remain without the solid manufacturing base of the kind possessed by the newly industrialized countries. Without such a base, a nation is an economic paraplegic, unable to cope with disaster or crisis, whether natural or man-made. The abject helplessness with which we responded to the earthquake, and the disarray with which we are responding to the Middle East conflict, demonstrate the inherent brittleness of an essentially agrarian economy. Our crisis is directly traceable to the self-destructive character of our development policies and, ultimately, to the forces responsible for those policies. Those policies have kept us from developing the productive capabilities and systemic efficiency of industrialized economies, and preserved us essentially as an agrarian state overwhelmingly dependent on imports and loans to keep the economy functioning. So, if for any reason, sources of loans dry up, imports correspondingly drop and the nation faces economic paralysis, acute, extensive shortages, and price spiral while unemployment mounts. Chaos becomes only a matter of time. And all for failure to industrialize.

To understand the process by which we reached this ultimate predicament, we need only compare the character and thrust of our economic programmes with that of the newly industrialized states of Asia, the most prominent of which are South Korea, Taiwan and India. A common denominator that binds those countries is the rigid discipline they exercise over the use of their foreign exchange and the obsession with which they have pursued a programme of industrialization within highly protected internal markets. Theirs are entirely controlled and centrally disciplined economies where spending on imports of non-essentials, and even on essentials already produced by domestic industries, are kept to a bare minimum, and where government assumes an intensely activist role in the process of economic modernization and industrialization.

The Philippines, on the other hand, has followed a diametrically opposite course. We have been doing everything that those countries refuse to do; and refuse to do what those countries insist on doing. We have opened our doors generously to imports, while they maintain what are basically closed economies; we have dismissed industrialization as a serious object of policy, while they made that the centerpiece of their economic programmes; we have relentlessly pursued the ideal of free trade, abjuring protectionism as though it were a heresy while they embraced protectionism as a cornerstone of policy, and rejected free trade as subversive of their interest We have made agriculture the focus of policy while they lavished their commitments on industry.

Facts and figures substantiate these observations.

1-- Since 1973, the year after martial law was declared, we have squandered more than $15 Billion on items classified as non-essentials and luxuries. Our import of these on an annual basis represents 21% of our total imports. An NIC, like South Korea, on the other hand, has spent no more than $1.5 Billion on non-essentials since 1973, and its annual import of non-essentials represents a bare 1.3% of its total annual import;[1] **(1. World Development Report)**

2. While the newly industrialized states continue to resist the heavy handed pressure exerted by the U.S. and the IMF/WB for them to remove restrictions on imports, the Philippines has gone overboard to accommodate the pressure. The decision of Estanislao of Finance and Paderanga of NEDA, to reduce tariffs to a maximum level of 30%, and their commitment to eliminate all direct restrictions on imports, reflect the government's embrace of free trade, and its repudiation of economic protectionism;

3. On declaration of martial law, the Philippines delisted from its development priorities the integrated steel, petrochemical and other heavy industries, and has since rejected the goal of developing the kind of heavy manufacturing complex that underlies the economies of the newly industrialized states?

4. Senator Vicente T. Patemo, chairman of the Senate Committee on Economic Affairs, admitted that while Chairman of the BOI during martial law, he made sure that industry took a subordinate position to agriculture in the government's priorities?

5. Senate majority floor leader Teofisto Guingona last year noted in a privilege speech that the country's development plans do not provide for an integrated steel industry, prompting editorial comment in media that Guingona's disclosure "could only mean that we have written off the long-term plan for industrialization in favor of perpetuating the present agricultural economy which, according to a United Nations report gives for the greatest efforts the least return to the worker outside of domestic servants."[4] (4--See Philippine Journal editorial, Oct. 25,1989.)

6. The truth is that the integrated steel industry has been delayed for the last 30 years, according to Antonio Arizabal, former secretary of the Department of Science and Technology?

7. As added evidence of the government's deliberate policy to avoid industrialization, when the NEDA's development plan was submitted to the consultative group of creditors at the meeting in Tokyo in 1987, no less than the Japanese

delegation criticized the plan on the ground that it had excessively concentrated on agricultural and rural development while completely overlooking the needs of industries;*

**** [2] **Times Journal, Jan. 28, 1973.**
[3] **Business Day, Oct. 7, 1982.**
[4] **See Philippine Journal editorial, Oct. 25,1989.**
[5] **Manila Bulletin, Sept 11,1989.** ****

8. Over the period 1965 to 1987, the Philippine manufacturing sector registered the lowest average annual growth rate in ASEAN, reflective of the government's policy of deliberate neglect towards industrialization during the period. Note the average annual growth rate of South Korea's manufacturing sector which explains that country's swift rise to NIC status, ahead of any ASEAN member.

	1965 80	1980 87
South Korea	18.7%	10.6%
Malaysia	n.a.	6.3%
Thailand	11.2%	6.0%
Indonesia	12.0%	7.0%
Singapore	13.2%	3.3%
Philippine	7.5%	1.1%

The figures should immediately dispel two other current notions on the cause of crisis. These are:

Corruption, nepotism and cronyism. - Among all notions this is perhaps the most dominant, and it has led to a constant, futile search for the "Mr. and Ms. Cleans" of this country. Since 1946, when we conducted our first national elections as a republic, this is the issue that has dominated virtually all presidential campaigns.

The figures on comparative economic performance, however, demolish this notion. In Indonesia, corruption, nepotism and cronyism have been rampant since Sukarno's time in the 1960s, and continue to be routine phenomena under the present military regime of Suharto. And the same goes for Thailand, where military coups have been as regular, and almost as routine, as corruption. Malaysia hasn't exactly been a nation governed by saints.

**** [6] Business Day, Feb. 12, 1987.
* World Development Report 1989. ****

Indonesia, however, recently offered to teach us how to manufacture aircrafts when the best we can do is produce midget bicycles and assemble overpriced cars out of manufactured components imported at an overprice. That country promises to emerge as the economic power of Southeast Asia by the end of this decade.

Malaysia and Thailand are concededly on the way to NIC status. Both have developed the nucleus of a heavy manufacturing complex, which here is virtually anathema.

Overpopulation. -This is a notion that is currently gaining ground. The absurdity of it becomes transparent when we recall that back in the time of the Commonwealth, our population was only some 15 million. But mass poverty was already a problem then, and produced a series of revolts in Central Luzon. The remedy for our economic predicament obviously doesn't lie in the mass murder of unborn infants.

One should also recall that, before the war, Japan was supposed to suffer from overpopulation, which explained if not justified her occupation of China. Today, the Japanese government is concerned that the country doesn't have enough people to sustain the manpower requirements of development.

The honest explanation for our crisis must lie, and can only lie, in the failure of policy. Our policies have obviously been designed to deny us the development which our neighbors now enjoy to an increasing degree.

And our people must be told, why and how that has come about.

For we deal with treason. Treason, not necessarily as that crime is narrowly defined in our criminal statutes; but treason in its broad and contemporary application, connoting betrayal of a nation's self-evident and declared interest. That is the social cancer that should be identified and excised before we can even plan on surviving an approaching cataclysm unleashed by that betrayal.

Until the respectable elements of this society display the honesty to confront that betrayal, and the system that nourishes and even rewards it, there can be no peace, and there should be no peace. Because justice, which alone can bring peace, must begin with the search for the roots of this nation's betrayal.

I. House Joint Resolution No. 2 as a Basis for the Charge of Economic Sabotage and Treason

To appreciate this charge, one must recall that in 1969 Congress met in extraordinary session to draft an alternative programme of government. The nation then was engulfed in crisis brought about by decontrol programme of 1962. That programme, financed and made possible by the IMF/WB and the U.S. government, dismantled the foreign exchange control system that had enabled our Central Bank to manage directly the nation's disbursements of dollars and to subject those disbursements to a rigorous test of priorities. Under that system, the importation of non-essential items as well as of items that were being produced by local industries, were either banned or quantitatively limited. Dollar remittances for over-[1] seas investments were prohibited, and the right of foreign companies to ship their profits out and withdraw their capital was tightly controlled. Flawed as it was, and vulnerable to abuse, that system enabled the nation to restrict the outflow of dollars and to confine that outflow largely for development purposes and social necessities. It was owing to that system that this country emerged at the end of the 1950s as the leading economic force in Southeast Asia with an economic structure that was discernibly headed towards NIC status.

The dismantlement of that system in 1962 set us on the road to the debt trap and bankruptcy. From then on, we began squandering our scarce dollar resources on imports that had absolutely no connection with development, including race horses, fighting cocks, Hollywood stars and basketball players. Worse still, we allowed and, in fact, encouraged the extensive outflow of investment capital. From that year began the steady accumulation by Filipinos of real estate assets and other forms of investment abroad.

Import liberalization and capital flight, along with devaluation, the three main ingredients of decontrol, logically led the country to its first major crisis since World War II. That crisis paved the way for the rise of Marcos, and, eventually, martial law.

The insistence of Marcos to continue with decontrol led, by 1968, to open speculations of a second devaluation, even as the nation plunged deeper into crisis.

The business community by then had begun clamoring for the reinstitution of the foreign exchange control system that the decontrol programme had lifted.

Because the Marcos administration persisted with decontrol, in the face of the mounting crisis, dollar outflow and shortage, the leadership of Congress decided to act on its own and to wrest the policy initiative from Malacanang. Meeting in a joint extraordinary session, Congress adopted an alternative economic programme drafted by the office of then Speaker Jose B. Laurel, Jr. The programme called for the effective repudiation of decontrol, the reinstitution of the foreign exchange control system, and a programme of industrialization.

That alternative programme was embodied in House Joint Resolution No. 2, otherwise known as the Magna Carta of Social Justice and Economic Freedom.

It is necessary to recall the Magna Carta because that document provides one of the bases for the charge made in this letter.

The Magna Carta legislated certain objectives of state as well as policies required to achieve those objectives. That document was forged in the anvil of a crisis whose main elements persist to this day in a much larger, and more explosive, dimension. We were then, as now, squandering scarce dollar resources on luxuries, financing that prodigality with borrowed funds, swamping the nation with imports that decimated local industries, permitting capital flight, allowing the peso to erode, resorting to draconian measures of monetary and credit restraint, and creating widespread unemployment and a price spiral in the process.

Congress wrestled with the cause of crisis and among the conclusions it drew was that the crisis was essentially rooted in an economy that had failed to industrialize. The decision was accordingly made to legislate industrialization as a paramount objective of state. Along with that objective, the Magna Carta also legislated a number of policies calculated to bring that objective to fruition. Among these was a programme of austerity to be enforced by the reinstitution of the foreign exchange control system that would, among others, ban the importation of luxuries.

I cite, Mr. Secretary, pertinent provisions of that document:

- Every encouragement shall be given by the Government to Filipino businessmen and investors to establish and operate basic and integrated industries essential to change the structure of our economy, substantially minimize our dependence on imports of raw materials, semi-processed goods and machinery and equipment, alter the quality and increase the value of our exports, provide greater job opportunities at better wages, and achieve a higher rate of economic growth. (Section on Paramount objectives of Economic Policy, par. 3).

Austerity and self-reliance are among the keystones to progress and national greatness. Conspicuous consumption and the ostentation of wealth are an assault on the social conscience and should be avoided by all, for they are censured by the whole nation.

The disposition of the nation's foreign exchange shall be subjected to a rigorous system of priorities and the importation of items that are hot essential to the nation's sound x x x development shall be subjected to tariff and to quantitative and/or qualitative measures. (Section on National Commitment to Austerity and Self-Reliance, par. 1 and 2).

If there is any doubt on what the Magna Carta intended, one needs only recall the speech that sponsored and launched it. That speech explained the reasons, purpose and goals of the resolution, and was delivered by the man on whose initiative Congress had convened in an atmosphere of crisis.

No less than the speaker of the House, Jose B. Laurel, Jr., sponsored the Magna Carta, and he stepped down from the speaker's rostrum to urge his colleagues to adopt it as the nation's policy masterplan and alternative programme of government. In so doing, he gambled the entire weight and prestige of his office, and political career, on that one single document. Had the document been rejected, it would have meant his political disgrace. He assumed the sole and entire burden of defending each and every provision of the resolution on the floor, before the searching scrutiny and even cynicism of a House which knew that the document which it was being called upon by its speaker to endorse constituted open war with the power in Malacanang.

The document was no less dramatic than the occasion, for it reflected a Congress in rebellion against the exactions of international finance, exactions which our chief executives, almost without exception, seemed unable to resist. But because Congress rose as one, on the nation's behalf, Malacanang was compelled to yield. On August 4,1969, Marcos signed the Magna Carta into law. It has since then remained the binding economic philosophy of the land.

I will quote extensively from the Laurel speech, Mr. Secretary, because it illuminates with blinding clarity the economic philosophy to which all governments of this country are bound in loyalty. That speech not only elucidated on what the document stands for, but equally elucidated the economic philosophy it was repudiating. It was unquestionably the most significant document to have emerged from Congress since we assumed political nationhood because it was in effect our people's declaration of economic independence.

First, the speech, characteristic of that clan, paid tribute to the memory of a late father whose political lifetime had been committed to the service of country.

I recall him because it was his dream that politics might one day transcend petty factionalism and unite our people in a resolute search for lasting solutions to our pressing social and economic difficulties.

He was particularly obsessed, as some other leaders of his time were, by the demanding challenges of economic development and social justice. He had warned repeatedly that unless we planned and planned well the life of this nation, its colonial, agro-merchandising economy, coupled with a severe imbalance in the way the wealth is distributed would spawn problems that could eventually engulf us all.

Laurel was in fact invoking the wisdom of the past. His late father was but a link in a long chain of national leaders who, as early as the first decade of this century, perceived that unless the country industrialized, independence would be hollow. Among them were: Juan Sumulong, the acknowledged brain of the opposition during the autocratic regime of Quezon, and grandfather of President Aquino on her mother's side; Quezon himself, president during the Commonwealth period, who conceived of the National Development Corporation (NDC), as government's instrument of industrialization and who, as Resident Commissioner to Washington, led the opposition against free trade which the U.S. congress legislated as the basis of Philippine-American relations. Quezon voiced the vigorous objection of the Philippine National Assembly to free trade on grounds that it would prevent the industrialization of the country. That was way back in 1909. Industrialization was pursued by Osmena, who succeeded Quezon as Commonwealth president, and who opposed free trade on similar grounds; by Manuel Roxas, first president of the Republic who, before the war, was one of the founding fathers of the National Economic Protectionism Association; by Elpidio Quirino who, as president, launched an economic mobilization programme to galvanize the nation towards industrial development; by Carlos P. Garcia, of the famed Filipino First Policy, whose administration made the decision for government to establish an integrated steel mill in order to hasten full industrialization; by the supreme nationalist, Claro M. Recto, whose brief for heavy industries remains unequalled in depth and comprehension. Even Diosdado Macapagal, whose administration gave the nation the ill-advised decontrol programme, was a firm believer in industrialization. He worked for the materialization of the integrated steel mill earlier decided on by his predecessor. He believed, although erroneously, that the system of protective tariffs, which he installed in place of controls which he had lifted, would be sufficient to spur the nation's industries.

Marcos, as this letter will show, believed that the nation should industrialize, and industrialize quickly, and he took actual steps to execute his idea.

There isn't a single president on record who opposed industrialization as a national goal although it wasn't until 1969 that that goal was elevated as a statutory and mandatory objective of state.

In the private sector, the need and urgency for industrialization was no less felt than in government. The industrialization movement, which started before the war with the founding of NEPA, blossomed in the 1950s with the organization of the Philippine Chamber of Industries (PCI) and the emergence of industrialist-statesmen, led by Salvador Araneta and Larry Henares, both of whom would produce a cascade of nationalist writings, along with numerous families, such as the Jacintos, Santiagos, Syjucos, Marcelos, Puyats, Sorianos, Delgados, Carloses, Aguinaldos, Felizardos, Teodoros, Madrigals, and many others too numerous to recall, who founded their respective business dynasties on the strength of incentives given them by government during the protectionist decade of the 1950s. Had it not been for their pioneering efforts, this country today would likely be as backward as some of the impoverished states of Africa, who have no industries to speak of.

But to turn to Laurel and his speech sponsoring the Magna Carta.

As he would proceed:

Many of our social problems spring from an archaic social structure that is unable to meet the employment requirements of 37 million people, growing at the rate of almost 3.5% a year. It is an economic structure marked by the conspicuous absence of a significant manufacturing capability and dependent mainly on agricultural pursuits as the largest source of the country's income and employment opportunities. What then was the remedy?

Only by industrializing the economy through the establishment of basic industries, particularly those that will utilize indigenous raw materials, can we hope to resolve the perennial problems of mass unemployment and marginal income that hound the lives of our people.

Mr. Secretary, those words were uttered twenty years ago, when our population was only 37 million, and when our external debt only $600 million. But at the time, our people already felt deeply the pangs of crisis, sufficiently enough to have moved their representatives to take the unprecedented step of wresting the policy initiative which, belonging to them in theory, had in practice lodged in Malacanang.

As Laurel would continue:

Ours today is essentially an agricultural economy with the industrial sector playing a minor role in terms of productivity. Even if we were to increase the products of our farms, we could never hope to fully absorb the mounting number of our unemployed. It is clear that the real solution to our unemployment problem lies in the systematic and organized pursuit of industrialization.

Coupled with the need to industrialize and provide maximum employment opportunities is the need to infuse technology in the lives of our people. Industrialization should not be confined to a few sectors of the economy. Economic policy should reflect a deliberate effort to bring to the mainstream of modern life the great number of our rural communities which time seems to have passed by. We must salvage them from

the torpor of backwardness and stagnancy and introduce to their inhabitants technological skills that will considerably raise their level of productivity.

In the context of the Magna Carta and the speech sponsoring it, it is clear that any economic programme which deviates fundamentally from its philosophy, objectives and thrust of policies constitutes economic sabotage. It is economic sabotage, and of the highest order, because the document deals with nothing less than the acknowledged imperatives of economic survival. It was no ordinary legislation. It was legislation compelled by crisis and has become even more compelling.

Behind the document was almost a year of extensive public hearings, when public hearings were taken seriously. And it was passed by a Congress whose composition reflected a brilliancy, independence and high mindedness that today has yet to be approximated.

In the upper chamber, the document was reported out and steered to acceptance by the Senate Committee on Economic Affairs. That committee was headed by no less than the late Jose W. Diokno whose intellect, courage, vision and foresight are now legend. As Laurel did in the lower House, Diokno defended the Magna Carta on the floor. Among his peers, there were Benigno Aquino, Jr. now a martyr; Salvador Laurel, now Vice President; Jovito Salonga, now Senate President; Dominador Aytona, former Finance Secretary; Ernesto Maceda, now chairman of the Senate Committee on National Defense; Ambrosio Padilla, a former Solicitor General and member of the Constitutional Commission; Arturo Tolentino, the durable parliamentarians' parliamentarian; the late Gil Puyat, the nation's foremost economist-industrialist at the time, and the late Gerardo Roxas, then president of the Liberal Party.

In the House, there were Speaker Laurel himself and Justiniano N. Montano, then minority floor leader, unquestionably among the most skillful parliamentarians produced by this country; former Speaker ComelioT. Villareal, Joaquin Roces, Jose Yap, now chairman of the House Committee on National Defense, and a host of others too many to name here.

Technically assisting in the crafting of that document were Dr. Isagani Cruz, now Associate Justice of the Supreme Court, and Dr. Emmanuel Q. Yap, who organized the economic staff of the Speaker and of the House and served as the first Director-General of the Congressional Economic Planning Office (CEPO) which assisted Laurel draft the resolution in consultation with the private sector.

What I am saying, Mr. Secretary, is that the Magna Carta is not a document to be taken lightly. In terms of its vital content, the circumstances that produced it, the urgency of the purpose that moved it, and the quality of the men and women who authored it, that document ranks second only to the Constitution in weight. In one respect, it is even weightier than the Constitution for it dealt with the very problem of this nation's survival, at a time when the nation felt its survival in jeopardy. What it said was that for the nation to survive, it must abide by certain objectives and policies. By implication, it said that failing in that, the nation could not survive. To undermine the essentials of the Magna Carta, therefore, would be to undermine the very security and survival of the state; and to betray its most vital and most obvious interest.

Vital, because what can be more vital than economic survival? Obvious, because what can be more obvious than that the survival of any modern state depends on its entry into the industrial age? If proof were needed for this, one needs only compare our condition with that of the Asian NICs. Because we are not industrialized, we cannot even cope with an earthquake or a typhoon, much less anticipate them. NICs, like South Korea and Taiwan, on the other hand, can even thrive on crisis, and with hardly any natural resources to speak of.

So crucial and imperative was the state objective legislated by the Magna Carta that even after Marcos had dissolved Congress, he never lost sight of the document's overriding objective. He saw the enduring validity of its central proposition: that the nation must industrialize if it is to survive. The Magna Carta was founded on that imperative. The very security of the state, military and not only economic, ultimately depends on that. Even social justice depends on that.

In this space and nuclear age, a nation that is not industrialized is an economic paraplegic that counts for nothing in the intensely competitive community of nations. It might as well be transported back to the Dark Age. Even its military establishment can only be a standing joke because it must depend even for its boots and shoe polish on others.

It is not a coincidence that the two most dynamic NICs in Asia, South Korea and Taiwan, were propelled to their spectacular condition by political leaders of military background: Park Chung Hee, and Chiang Kai Shek. Because more so than the civilian mind, the military easily grasps the strategic value of industrialization, particularly an industrialization based on industries precisely contemplated by the Magna Carta: industries that would make a nation self-sufficient in machineries and industrial raw materials; industries founded on steel and metals. This was the reason why Park defied the IMF/WB when those agencies, in 1970, counseled him against establishing a steel industry because he saw, as a military man, the strategic relation between national self-sufficiency, national defense and steel. One, after all, does not produce armaments out of rice and vegetables, or machines out of paper, or ships out of plastic. To Park, the steel industry was important not for the number of people that it could employ, but for the strategic material it represented. To develop the capacity to produce that strategic material was worth the cost, any cost. And events vindicated him.

Another country much closer to home that is frantically trying to industrialize is Indonesia, a nation also led by a sagacious militarist who realizes the economic-military value of an industrialization based on the heavy industries.

The steel industry is not only the mother of industries. It is in the essence of national security.

Industrialization as an objective of state even during

Martial Law. This was what Marcos grasped. That was why in 1976 he pressed for the speedy implementation of an integrated steel mill that had been on the drawing board since 1958, and three years thereafter directed the installation of 11 major industrial projects. By 1979, he had begun to panic because he saw that South Korea and Taiwan had sprinted beyond reach in the developmental race. South Korea began the construction of her steel, engine and machine industries as early as 1969, while Taiwan did so in the mid-seventies. And so Marcos, not to be outdone, in 1979 formally announced a programme that would give the nation the projects needed to launch the country into the industrial age by early 1980s.

In launching the 11 major industrial projects, he warned: If we do not shift gears and get on the same fast track (as our neighbors) we would not be able to catch up and shall be left to receive the dust of those we follow. (FM Launches 11 major projects, Philippine Daily Express, September 29,1979).

He reiterated his determination to accelerate the country's industrialization in a speech before the Philippine Business Conference two months later, on November 1979.

Since the day we regained our independence in 1946 and began our march towards modem nationhood, we have been repeatedly cautioned by economists of various persuasion against adopting over-ambitious industrialization program.

I believe that such words of caution have lost their validity for us today if indeed they had any validity at all in the past.

XXX

And committing himself to a program of full industrialization, he said:

I believe this task cannot be achieved without a full industrialization program. And that is what we are talking about. (Economic Policies and Direction, Philippine Daily Express, Nov. 21, 1979).

That was what the Magna Carta had urged ten years earlier.

This is no brief for Marcos, Mr. Secretary, because it is on record that I was part of the opposition during martial law. As a matter of fact, your Department was one of the agencies that issued the warrant for my arrest as a political prisoner. But the facts must be respected and it was fact that he did attempt, by word and deed, to at least establish the nucleus of an industrial program and to get industrialization off the ground. It is necessary to recount Marcos' own struggle to industrialize the economy because it established the fact that industrialization, as a state objective, did not cease to be a state objective when he dissolved Congress and declared martial law. In fact, as Marcos action showed, it assumed even more urgency. And it did not cease to be an objective of state with the passing of Marcos because President Aquino, after her trip to mainland China, has repeatedly expressed the hope of seeing the Philippines transform into an NIC.

Indeed, what head of state would turn his or her back on industrialization? What people, for that matter? It is the ambition of every Third World country to become an NIC. Asia has become the seat of the developmental drama precisely because of its NICs: China, Taiwan, South Korea and Singapore; as well as of its emerging NICs: Indonesia, Malaysia, Thailand, North Korea, and even Vietnam. Each of these, with the exception of Singapore whose 2.5 million population is obviously too small to warrant one, now has a functioning integrated steel industry.

To industrialize is an aspiration that is as natural and instinctive to every developing nation-state as to learn and to be able to walk about and run are aspirations that come naturally and instinctively to every normal child. It is an aspiration that need not even be legislated as a state objective, and anyone who opposes it can only be moved by unnatural feelings.

This being so, how explain the state of the nation? If, at least since 1969, industrialization has been a legislated objective of state, why is it that we have failed to make even a token motion towards that direction? How explain the anti-industrialization thrust of our policies? How is it that the steel industry has been delayed for thirty years? How explain that the development plan of this country, as pointed out by Senator Guingona, has no provision for the development of an integrated steel industry? How explain that Marcos, the dictator that he was, could not get his industrial projects off the ground? How come, when our government submitted its economic plan to the Consultative Group of Creditors in 1987, no less than the Japanese delegation had to remind our panel that the plan was unrealistic because it had completely overlooked the requirements of industries?

To ask these questions is to answer them. Is it not plain, Mr. Secretary, that the state objective has been undermined by the very functionaries who had been, and continue to be, entrusted with the economic policies of the country?

We shall take them one by one. Virata was the arch technocrat of the Marcos years and is generally regarded as the man principally behind the nation's loan programmes and policies. Negotiations on the loans incurred by the Marcos government were almost single-handedly conducted by Virata. In fact, his role as loan negotiator was virtually one of the conditions demanded by the IMF/WB. The conditionalities he accepted ultimately determined the state of the economy.

What was Virata's economic philosophy?

Early in his public career, in 1970, at a commencement speech before the faculty and graduating class of the Philippine Normal College, Virata went on record that he considered industrialization, along with socialism, a dangerous idea. For that, he was immediately taken to task by media who described him as a man "who has run out of his senses." (See "Virata Lists 6 Danger Concepts", Manila Chronicle, April 22, 1970; "Development Trends", Business Day, April 24,1970)

That was less than a year after the Magna Carta had been signed into law.

Virata headed the team of negotiators in February 1970 who committed the Philippines to the floating rate. An integral part of the conditionalities was that the Philippines, aside from allowing the peso to devalue, should refrain from exchange controls. That particular conditionality constituted the first open defiance of avital principle embodied in the Magna Carta.

The negotiators didn't even bother to consult Congress, and not even Marcos appears to have been consulted. The negotiators returned from Washington and simply confronted the political authorities and the nation with an accomplished fact. It took a Senate hearing to elicit from them the conditionalities to which they had agreed.

Only two months earlier, in December 1969, a recently re-elected Marcos reiterated a pledge he had made during the presidential campaign, that he would not consent to the devaluation of the peso, and that if the IMF were to insist on it his government would consider seceding from that organization. (Business Day, December 26, 1969).

Virata's economic philosophy, which he expressedin 1970, explains why the first investment priorities plan which the BOI (of which he was then chairman) submitted in 1968 was rejected by the National Economic Council (NEDA's predecessor agency) on the particular ground that it was manifestly biased against industries that would facilitate the country's industrialization. (Manila Times, May 18, 1968).

When Marcos announced his major industrial projects in 1979, the World Bank immediately sought its deferment, and Virata supported the World Bank on that move (Times Journal, Nov. 20,1981; see also Metro Manila Times, September 26,1985).

Virata, together with former NEDA head Dr. Gerardo Sicat and former BOI Chairman Vicente T. Patemo, constituted the economic triumvirate during the main part of martial law which shaped the nation's economic direction, undermined the country's industrialization, and started the country on the road to Free Trade in open contravention of the Magna Carta.

Former NEDA Head Gerardo Sicat

If Virata negotiated the loans of the Marcos government, Gerardo Sicat, who was appointed NEDA head just before martial law, designed the theoretical frame of the country's anti-industrialization strategy.

The role of this particular functionary in undermining the country's industrialization started while he was still an assistant professor at the U.P. School of Economics. He was perhaps the first, if not the only, economist from academe at the time to have opposed the policies enunciated by the Magna Carta. From his professorial seat at the U.P., he issued statements opposing protectionism, the reinstitution of the foreign exchange control system, and the industrialization of the type proposed by Congress. He contended that the position paper submitted by the CEPO (Congressional Economic

Planning Office) which had provided the Speaker's office with technical support, overdramatized the unemployment and inflation problems, which by the late '60s had driven the nation to crisis.

Then in 1972, Sicat published a book containing a collection of his writings in which he had proposed that the country abandon economic protectionism altogether as well as any plans for industries, like steel and petrochemicals, that require the extensive use of machines. The country, he theorized, should concentrate its developmental programme on light industries, geared to the export market, that require (a) minimal use of capital and machine power and (b) maximum use of labor power. To Sicat, it wasn't enough that the government had eliminated through the 1962 decontrol programme all direct restriction on imports and foreign exchange transactions. He contended that even tariffs should be eliminated, along the ways of Hong Kong, and attributed the economic crisis then to the tariff system. He was father to the idea that local industries should be subjected to the unlimited competition of imports because such competition allegedly would force domestic industries to be competitive in the world market. That idea was to develop into a doctrine which a long line of professors from the U.P. School of Economics, the more prominent of whom are Solita Monsod and Cayetano Paderanga, would assiduously espouse. That view underlies the import liberalization program of the Aquino government, of which EO 413, which would reduce tariffs to a maximum of 30%, is the latest, but by no means the ultimate, stage.

Sicat's writings, by his own admission, were financed jointly by the Rockefeller Foundation and the U.P. School of Economics. (See Acknowledgements in his book, Economic Policy and Philippine Development).

Former BOI Chairman Vicente T. Patemo

If Virata handled the loan negotiations of the Marcos government and yielded only too easily to the IMF conditionalities, and if Sicat designed the theoretical framework ofthe anti-industrialization strategy, Patemo, in his long tenure as BOI Chairman, executed that strategy.

Soon after martial law. was declared, Patemo as BOI Chairman, delisted the steel, petrochemical and other basic industries from the priority list of that agency (Times Journal, January 22, 1973). That act was an open declaration of war against the Magna Carta. Steel and the other heavy industries (otherwise referred to as capital-intensive) had been included in the priority list of the BOI following the National Economic Council's criticism in 1968 of the first BOI plan, and the Magna Carta's passage into law in 1969.

When martial law was declared, Paterno obviously took it on himself to delist the basic industries, thereby depriving them of investment incentives and effectively announced that insofar as his strategic office was concerned, industrialization had ceased to be a state objective.

There is ground for holding that Paterno acted on his own because in 1976, Marcos issued a directive to the Iron and Steel Authority, which Paterno then headed, directing that agency to speed up the implementation of the integrated steel mill.

(Bulletin Today, July 15,1976). Apparently, as far as Marcos , was concerned, the steel industry still commanded the official priority of his government, and that he had never intended to abandon plans for that industry.

Three years after, in 1979, an obviously frustrated Marcos announced a programme for the speedy industrialization of the country through 11 major industrial projects, led by steel, which still remained on the planning board. By that time, Patemo had already been replaced as BOI Chairman by Roberto Ongpin, on whose shoulders fell the task of implementing the Marcos industrialization directive. Marcos had obviously tired of Patemo.

Considering that an integrated steel mill had in fact been an economic priority of this country since 1958, when the Garcia administration officially made it a policy to establish one, the delay of that industry can be attributed only to the BOI which has been in operation since 1968, and which was precisely constituted to foster the industrialization of the country. Patemo was the longest-serving chairman of that agency.

Like Virata, however, Patemo from the start already displayed an active hostility toward the industry. In fact, it was during his incumbency that national restiveness over the delay of such a vital project began to surface. That restiveness was expressed in an editorial of the Business Day in its issue of July 4, 1972, I quote extensively from that editorial:

Why the delay?

The Presidential Steel Committee seems to be taking its own sweet time deciding on the establishment of a blast furnace.

Board of Investments Governor Conrado Sanchez yesterday said this is due to the government's desire to rationalize the steel industries.

The Committee's target, he explained, is to make a review of the proposed blast furnace by 1975, the production capacity of which will be tailored to the requirements of the steel industry.

This major announcement by the Governor is something of a revelation. Earlier, the government had been stressing the need for the establishment of basic industries.

The Committee's decision seems to imply that a blast furnace is not important in the Philippine economy and therefore, there is no need to establish it immediately.

Or, is the government's decision meant to discourage Iligan Integrated Steel Mills, Inc. from pursuing its planned backward integration?

It is a recognized fact that the country's steel industries have to be rationalized since there is overcrowding in certain steel industry sectors like fabrication.

But this should not be made at the expense of ignoring the immediate and most important goal of producing steel from the country's iron ores.

The Philippines is already behind in its establishment of a blast furnace. The delay will seriously hamper and undermine the ability of the country to be self-sufficient in steel, a major material in industrialization.

If the government does not want Iligan Integrated Steel Mill to set up a blast furnace then this must be indicated immediately. The alternative should already be provided.

Right now, the fabrication industries continue to depend heavily on Japan for various intermediate steel products. At the same time, shipments of Philippine iron ores to Japan are not growing fast enough, considering that country's growing inventory of raw materials.

The Presidential Steel Committee has legitimate objectives in trying to force steel industries to integrate production and achieve economies of scale. There is a considerable reason to believe that the ability of the government to rationalize the steel industries will redound to a better planning of the production output of the blast furnace.

But time is of the essence. The Committee seems unwilling to support the blueprint prepared by IISMI for its blast furnace. This has been indicated by BOI Chairman Vicente T. Paterno in several instances.

If the projected capacity is not viable, the Steel Committee or the Board can perhaps prepare, at this stage, an alternative plan.

Up to now, the iron and steel industry seems to be the most ignored segment of the Philippine economy, notwithstanding the fact that it is already composed of 40 steel melting and rolling plants, two tinning plants, eight galvanizing plants, 20 fabrication firms and about 118 steel foundries.

However, many of these industries don't have "viable" capacities because they are operating below economic levels due to high production costs.

The country is still heavily dependent on imports to the extent that at least 95 cent of intermediate steel products come from abroad.

This is one situation the government cannot ignore. Continued complacency on the blast furnace venture will only make us more dependent on Japan for steel product intermediaries.

The BOI, as chairman of the Presidential Steel Committee should review its position in relation to the blast furnace project. But if it is no longer interested in seeing the industry integrate backwards from its present scrap melting and fabrication activities, that is another story.

What was Patemo's response to that editorial?

Exactly one week after that editorial appeared, Paterno, then back from a trip to Indonesia, announced that he would recommend to Marcos an "Asean perspective" in the country*s development programme. Specifically, his suggestion was that capital-intensive industries, like steel and chemical, should be considered "Asean projects," which in his words, "need not be established in the Philippines," (see story of Amado Macasaet, Manila Times, July 11, 1972).

That was some three months before martial law was declared.

In that context, one sees that Patemo's decision to delist the basic industries from the BOI's priority was prompted primarily by an apparent commitment to some foreign government in the ASEAN that he would strive to defer the steel and other capital intensive projects in the Philippines, and to work for his government's approval to have them considered as ASEAN projects instead, which "need not be established in the Philippines."

His recommendation was obviously disapproved by Marcos, but the industry remained excluded from the government's priority after he had delisted it in 1973.

It was during Paterno's long tenure as BOI Chairman and Industry Secretary that the steel industry was subjected to an endless chain of dilatory "feasibility" studies. After Marcos, in 1979, declared a program to hasten the basic industries, he acidly remarked that "These projects are not new. We have been studying them for many years and for a number of them, for too many years." (see Asiaweek, June 6,1980).

Those who would seek an explanation for the essential reason why dictatorship in South Korea was attended by the dramatic industrialization of that country, while dictatorship in the Philippines was marked by outright stagnation, might recall that as early as 1970, South Korea, over the objections of the IMF/WB, proceeded with an integrated steel complex while, in the Philippines, such a complex was, through the action of Patemo, officially removed from the government's priorities.

As if to add insult to injuiy, in 1982, long after Patemo had ceased to be connected with the BOI, he admitted that while with that office, he had felt that industry should take a back seat to agriculture. Also that year, while a member of the Batasan, he expressed the view that Marcos' 11 industrial projects were premature and that it would be criminal to operate an industry like steel, considering the negligible employment opportunity it would open when compared with the extensive capital requirement it would entail.

Such was the man who served as BOI Chairman during the main part of martial law, the very agency entrusted to shape the character of the country's investment programmes.

No one could have sabotaged the country's industrialization more effectively than Paterno. And admission of sabotage was what his 1982 statements effectively add up to. Those admissions explain his motivation as the man charged with the task of implementing the industrialization program.

Between Virata, who determined the IMF conditionalities which this country would accept; Sicat, who provided the theoretical framework for an economic programme that would exclude the very industries that have made NICs of South Korea and Taiwan; and Patemo, who believed that the implementation of those industries would be untimely and "criminal" in the first place, and that industries should take the back seat to agriculture, Marcos' industrialization programme never stood a chance. For that matter, Magna Carta and the nation never stood a chance.

And so it was that we ended the decade of the 1970s with a foreign debt of some $15 Billion, and without any basic industry to show for it. In the meanwhile, South Korea and Taiwan had emerged from the shadows of underdevelopment with an industrial base from which to take off to NIC status. And that they would do in the ensuing decade, while we would sink deeper into the quicksand of the debt trap, an economic vegetable.

It was the decade of the 1970s that determined how we would fare in future, because it was that decade which determined whether we had the will to establish the real foundations of development as the Magna Carta had decreed we should.

South Korea and Taiwan did, as well as our neighbors in Southeast Asia. The Philippines, on the other hand, took the course of suicide. We built our foundation, not on the strength of metals and steel, but on imports that had nothing whatever to do with development, and on foreign debt to finance those imports and buy our way to bankruptcy. Had government abided by the instructions of the Magna Carta, we could count ourselves by now among the NICs of Asia.

Which takes us to the second aspect of the triumvirate's conspiracy.

The more vicious aspect of that conspiracy was directed against the Magna Carta's call for a programme of austerity through a system that would subject the nation's disbursement of dollars to a rigorous test of priorities and avoid the use of those dollars for luxuries.

The main thrust of the conspiracy was to commit, the Philippine to the free trade doctrine of the IMF/WB, the very doctrine repudiated by the Magna Carta. Consistent with that thrust, the triumvirate broke a long standing and long entrenched tradition against joining GATT, the world organization committed to absolute free trade. It was bad enough that decontrol had eliminated all direct restriction on imports, leaving only a tariff system to serve as an indirect method of discouraging foreign goods. But the triumvirate committed Philippine policy to the eventual elimination of tariffs when in 1975 it caused our accession to, or membership in, GATT.

The action of the triumvirate left no doubt that it intended to return this nation to the regime of absolute free trade such as what prevailed during the colonial period of the Commonwealth when we had neither import controls nor tariffs with which to protect ourselves from the unlimited invasion of imports.

That, in fact, was the theoretical model of Sicat. Sicat's policy blueprint called for the free trading colony of Hong Kong as the eventual Philippine model, and it is in this context that one must view the latest action of this government in proposing a maximum ceiling of 30% for Philippine tariffs. That would not be the last proposal of its kind.

The Magna Carta could not possibly have met a more open defiance. The free trade course to which the triumvirate was unmistakably steering Philippine policy represented the ultimate death blow to any plans for industrialization. Far more deadly than simply depriving industries, of any incentive whatsoever, was the plan to open up the domestic market unlimitedly to imports. Not even a super industrial power like Japan is prepared to conduct its international trade on the basis of how the Virata triumvirate conducted our nation's international transactions. Nor the United States. Nor the members of the ECC. Nor the Asian NICs. This is exactly what the savage US-Japan trade war, and the current round of international trade negotiations, are proving. If they have accomplished any purpose at all, those global negotiations have exposed the intricate and extensive mechanism of protective devices that the highly developed countries have contrived to protect their domestic industries from import aggression. And among these devices, tariffs are in fact the least important. The dominant and really effective weapons are the outright bans and quantitative quotas placed on imports, as well as the enormous subsidies extended by government to those industries whose exports they seek to promote. It is this type of protectionism that the Virata triumvirate agreed to dismantle. Not satisfied with that, it also committed to dismantle the tariff system.

Fortunately, within the Marcos administration, there was a faction which resisted the thrust of the Virata triumvirate. That faction was led by the late Gregorio Licaros, then governor of the Central Bank. Licaros refused to be bound by the commitments of the triumvirate, and that explains the residual protectionism which Philippine policy retained during the Marcos regime. Under that protectionism, imports of the more obvious non-essentials were either banned in practice or allowed, as in the case of fruits, only seasonally or in limited quantities. Agricultural goods were basically shielded from import competition. But the IMF persisted nonetheless in having import bans lifted even on items like chewing gum.

The International Monetary Fund is asking the Philippine government to eliminate all types of foreign exchange restrictions applied on commodities many of which are minor in importance.

One of the minor items that the IMF is seeking is the removal of Central Bank control over the importation of a non-essential such as chewing gum, according to Finance Secretary Cesar Virata in a recent interview. ("IMF involved in RP, from US dollars to import of gums." Times Journal, Jan. 12, 1978).

Notwithstanding the residual protectionism insisted on by Licaros the fundamental character of the nation's import policy, as shaped by the triumvirate, remained and prevailed.

It was essentially an open one, gradually but inexorably heading towards full elimination of all types or forms of import restraint, tariffs included. That objective, impeded by the Central Bank during the Marcos years, would eventually achieve a breakthrough under the Aquino government's programme of import-lib, as pressed, first by former NEDA chief Solita Monsod and the late Finance Secretary Jaime Ongpin and, subsequently, by their respective successors in office, Cayetano Paderanga and Jesus Estanislao.

Which takes us to the Aquino government, its economic philosophy and functionaries. Marcos and Aquino policies compared.

The basic difference between the Marcos and Aquino programmes lies essentially in the residual protectionism which the former had retained. That protectionism was represented by the import ban and restrictions that applied on a good number of items. Many of those items were obvious non-essentials and luxuries, and the ban on them, according to IMF/WB, constituted a violation of the conditionalities that our negotiators, namely, Virata, had agreed to.

The CB under Marcos had become somewhat of an impediment to the nation's march towards the absolute free trade, which Sicat had held out as the appropriate goal of policy, and to which Virata and Paterno steadily steered the country.

When the Aquino government assumed power, the CB's residual protectionism became the primary focus of attack, and that attack was led by Solita Monsod, the firstNEDAhead under the Aquino government and the late Jaime Ongpin, Aquino's first Finance Secretary. The CB, then headed by Fernandez, obviously was unable to ward off the attack of the free traders the way it had managed to do so under Marcos. Note that Fernandez was at the helm of the CB during the last years of Marcos, and one of his first statements when appointed to that post was that he would tighten on the imports of non-essentials.

If Virata, Sicat and Patemo constituted the triumvirate that led the assault on the objectives and policies of the Magna Carta during Marcos' time, the late Jimmy Ongpin, Solita Monsod and Fernandez became their counterpart in the first and decisive years of the Aquino government.

Former NEDA Head Solita Monsod

Monsod is actually one of the disciples of the Sicat school and, like Sicat, was a professor at the U.P. School of Economics when tapped for the post of NEDA chief. But, unlike Sicat, Monsod pushed the drive towards free trade to heights it had not reached during Marcos' time, and which would be pushed to even more elevated heights by her successor, Cayetano Paderanga.

It was Monsod, with the quiet support of Ongpin, who functioned as the battering ram of the free traders, and it was she who provided the theoretical ammunition with which to justify the elimination of the country's residual protectionism. In this, Monsod clashed with BOI's Concepcion. Monsod's drive to further liberalize our import policy in fact provided the first major issue that divided the Aquino cabinet.

Concepcion's opposition to further import liberalization was, expectedly enough, supported by the industrial sector. But it was the League of Provincial Governors, then headed by Bren Guiao, who provided the opposition to import-lib-with grassroots support. At the height of the import-lib controversy, the League petitioned Malacanang to suspend the liberalization programme on the ground that it would work havoc on livelihood in the countryside. President Aquino did suspend the programme for a time, but was eventually prevailed upon to lift the suspension. It was then that imports assumed ridiculous dimensions. Among the first items liberalized were hopia, beer, and marble statuettes. Soon, the country would be importing items like fish sauce (patis) from Vietnam, toothpaste from mainland China, furniture from Sweden, canned sugar cane juice from Singapore, ballpens from Spain, dairy products from Malaysia, chocolates from Switzerland, and a host of canned foods which the residual protectionism of the Marcos years had managed somehow to either restrain or ban altogether.

But if NEDA's import lib had its ridiculous diversions, it also brought its own tragedy. At no time in the history of this nation have farmers been victimized by import invasion the way they are being victimized now. In fact, before Monsod's time, the farmers were hardly heard to complain. The complaint against import invasion had been virtually confined to the industrial sector. In less than a year after Aquino assumed power, however, farmers' complaint against the government's import policy swelled like a flood. There is hardly any sector in the farm community which has not been heard to protest the nation's import programme.

While pressing for a full blown liberalization, Monsod simultaneously led the move for the devaluation of the peso. It was her voice that towered above the others in the crusade for a "realistic" peso-dollar rate. In this, however, she was only being faithful to the prescriptions of the school to which she belonged. One of the doctrinal mysteries of that school is the theory that a generous dose of imports, coupled with devaluation, would force domestic industries to be competitive in both the domestic and international market; and that, corrolarily, by protecting domestic industries, one encourages inefficiencies. Exactly the theory propounded by the IMF/WB.

This is a theory which, of course, defies economic reality. It defies the reality of highly, if not overly, protected economies like Japan, South Korea and Taiwan. A common element in the success of these Asian economic tigers is precisely the intensely protectionist character of their developmental policies. Highly developed as they are, their policies remain incomparably far more protectionist than ours.

As for the theory that devaluation renders exports more competitive it is almost truism that while that theory might apply to industrialized economies, it can only work havoc on economies dependent extensively on agricultural and raw material products for their export revenues, particularly when coupled with a highly permissive policy towards imports. Devaluation has only succeeded in making real estate and other assets in the Philippines increasingly attractive to foreign buyers.

NEDA's formula is far from original. We experimented with that formula as early as 1962, and the result was disaster. It was that disaster which provoked Congress to enact the Magna Carta.

Because of the import liberalization urged by Monsod and Ongpin, we squandered $1.2 Billion on luxuries in 1986, and that rose to $ 1.5 Billion in 1987. Figures for 1988 to 1990, when they? become available, I am sure would prove even more devastating. It is now generally acknowledged that our trade deficits largely stem from imports that have no bearing whatsoever on development.

The pressure exerted on us by the IMF/WB to open the floodgates to imports and devalue the currency have been incalculably reinforced, if not facilitated outright, by local functionaries pressing on the same theme.

It is important to recall the role of Monsod and Ongpin in the early years ofthe Aquino govemment because they reflected the basic continuity of the economic philosophy represented by the triumvirate of Virata, Sicat and Paterno. The torch which she and Ongpin inherited and carried on, would in turn be handed to Estanislao and Paderanga, by each successive instance, the economic philosophy they all bared would be applied with increasing fanaticism and callous disregard for its most obvious consequences. The Virata triumvirate was at least restrained by the residual protectionism ofthe Central Bank under Licaros. That residual protectionism was eliminated by Monsod and Ongpin. Estanislao and Paderanga would carry the torch further with their EO 413.

The inexorable progression towards absolute Free Trade by now should be plain and evident.

It was during Monsod's incumbency that the nation's development plan, presented in Tokyo in 1987 during the meeting with the Consultative Group of Creditors, was criticized by the Japanese delegation for overlooking the needs of industries and focusing its attention on agriculture.

But perhaps the most devastating criticism of the NEDA plan was the comment of Dr. Amado Castro, also of the U.P. School of Economics, which I quote hereunder:

Last week the view was expressed that the medium Term Development Plan, 1987-1992 prepared by NEDA suffers from the shortcoming that it lacks a long term vision of the Philippine economy. It was suggested that in the long term the objective should be to transform the Philippine economy into a more industrialized one. The medium term development plan does have a chapter on industry, trade and tourism. The fact that the three large sectors of the economy, plus a section on industrial peace, are lumped together whereas there are separate chapters on Agriculture and Natural Resources, is already indicative. It indicates that NEDA does not consider manufacturing an important enough sector meriting full discussion.

Dr. Castro proceeds to conclude:

Nowhere in the plan is it stated that an industrial revolution should take place in the Philippines as this is where the future lies. Agriculture simply cannot be the long-run engine of growth in this country. It cannot create all the jobs and the incomes that future and for that matter even present Filipinos need and deserve.

This neglect of manufacturing is disappointing. It shows that not enough thought was given to such a key segment of the economy. As was remarked last week, that is more than a pity; ultimately it is a major flaw in the NEDA plan. (Castro, "Economic Viewpoint," Sunday Times, April 5, 1987).

Monsod's plan was simply following the established bias of her predecessors against real industrialization, and explains Senator Guingona's observation that the development plan of the country does not include provision for an integrated steel industry.

Finance Secretary Jesus Estanislao, NEDA's Cayetano Paderanga and EO 413: The Real Meaning of EO 413.

If there is any doubt that this country has been pro-grammed since martial law to become another Hong Kong, in compliance with the IMF/WB-GATT doctrine of absolute free trade, that doubt has been put to rest by Estanislao and Paderanga, the two officials directly behind EO 413.

EO 413 virtually dismantles the system of protective tariffs with which we have lived since 1962. Pegging tariffs to a maximum of 30% effectively strips the tariff system of its protective function, and reduces it to a mere revenue-raising devise. Coupled with the outstanding commitment made by the Virata triumvirate to eliminate all remaining forms of direct import restraints, a commitment reiterated and implemented by Monsod and Ongpin, JEO 413 marks the formal and effective return of this country to the free trade regime of the Commonwealth, when government was power-less to protect domestic industries from imports either directly, through controls or, indirectly, through tariffs.

Mr. Secretary, even South Korea, whose economy is nearly five times ours, has refused to liberalize its market, and any functionary who would just as much as express views in favor of market or import liberalization is committing political suicide.

Following is a revealing account from the Asian Wall Street Journal's issue of November 12 this year:

U.S. officials are expressing increasing impatience with South Korea's reluctance to open its markets to foreign goods and services, signaling heightened trade friction in the months ahead.

The report went on to say:

The negotiating impasse last week was the latest of several recent examples of a broader trend that foreign officials and businesses are encountering in Korea. Foreign officials say the country is waging a campaign against imported goods by encouraging consumers not to spend on 'luxury items.' In addition, sentiment is strengthening in Korea against the Uruguay Round of multilateral talks on liberalizing global trade.

XXX

That angry mood among Koreans has made it politically suicidal for Korean officials who favor reform to speak out. A government official said privately that anyone in his ministry who expresses reformist views is hooted down. 'I think the overall environment has affected market liberalization,' Mr. Dallara said, ("Korea Stance on Market Stirs U.S. Impatience").

If there is anything that the current round of multilateral trade negotiations, known as the Uruguay Round, is proving, it is that even the highly developed nations will not be persuaded towards the kind of economic disarmament represented by Free Trade, notwithstanding the profusion of their rhetorical commitment to that philosophy.

In South Korea and Taiwan, functionaries like Estanislao and Paderanga would likely face charges of treason within twenty-four hours following announcement of a measure like EO 413. And such charge would be rooted in the logic and clear imperatives of modem warfare.

II. The Nature of Modern Warfare as a Basis for the Charge of Treason

Treason in essence consists in the giving of aid and

comfort to the enemies of the state, particularly in times of war. War, however, is not confined to the outbreak of armed hostilities.

Modem war is essentially economic in nature. In its modem application, it is a struggle for the conquest of markets: markets where one may sell, or dump, his goods and services; markets where raw materials may be extracted; markets where capital may derive super profits; and markets where human labor may be had cheaply.

With the advent of nation-states, military wars became largely the extension and projection of the war for markets. The U.S. provoked Spain into war in order to wrest from the latter the markets of Cuba and the Philippines. The Pacific war reflected the intense economic rivalry of the U.S. and Japan for the markets of Southeast Asia.

War, any war, is about markets.

This is a reality which apparently isn't taught at the U.P. School of Economics and the Center for Research and Communications (CRC) where Monsod, Paderanga and Estanislao were trained; institutions that today function as the organized bastions of the Free Trade doctrine.

If modern warfare is essentially a war for markets, then a philosophy that would compel a nation to open up its market by discarding the weapons of market protection automatically partakes of treason. If not treason, then what is it?

A state official who would persuade, if not maneuver, his government to drop the weapons of economic protection places himself in the analogous position of a functionary who would maneuver his country to disarm in the midst of armed conflict.

Bluntly, Mr. Secretary, that is the position into which the proponents of free trade or import liberalization, particularly of EO 413, have maneuvered themselves.

Their high crime is highlighted by two factors: one, is the rising tide of protectionism brought about by the condition of the world economy which is increasingly forcing nations to protect themselves from the repercussions of an international recession. The least that Estanislao and Paderanga could have done was to maintain existing levels of protection, low and inadequate as they are. And two, is the essence of th e IMF/WB doctrine, of which import liberalization is representative. That doctrine, Free Trade, has always constituted the economic basis of the colonial relation. That the IMF/WB should push for free trade is understandable. It was founded after all by the colonial powers, led by the U.S., France and England, to promote free trade on a global basis obviously to preserve the economic basis of the colonial relation indefinitely long after their colonies shall have acquired independence.

But for Third World economists to press free trade on their governments is something that cannot possibly be explained on normal grounds. It is simply unnatural.

The devastating consequences of Free Trade on any economy, whether developed or underdeveloped, are time proven. We have had direct experience with those consequences during the colonial period. We experimented with a modified version of free trade in 1962 and progressively since then, through decontrol. And the result was disaster, provoking Congress to enact the Magna Carta.

The fact that a super-industrial state like Japan refuses to open up to imports completely should convince even the untutored that free trade carries with it extreme danger, even for developed countries. The United States, for pursuing a policy that has displayed considerably less rigor than Japan's in the supervision of its imports, is heavily paying the price of import liberalization. The country which emerged after World War II as the foremost industrial power in the world is economically disintegrating before our eyes, flooded by massive imports from Japan, an economy which refuses to open up.

Perhaps it does take a military mind to really appreciate the strategic necessity of protecting a domestic market from the aggression of foreign imports as well as foreign capital. Such a mind cannot fail to grasp the essence of modern war, and the stratagem necessary to win that war. It is no coincidence that the powerful economies in Asia today, Japan, South Korea, Taiwan and China, have been shaped by protectionist policies, fashioned by leaders immersed in the tradition and outlook of the military. And it is no coincidence either that the man who originally designed the protectionist policies that led to the industrialization of the United States, began public service as a military aide to General Washington. Col.

Alexander Hamilton, we know, had nothing but contempt for Adam Smith and his disciples.

In this intensely competitive age of nation-states, to espouse Free Trade, which currently passes for NEDA's import-lib, is to walk the path of treason.

Economists of the First World might have their plausible reasons for wishing free trade on their country. But the Philippines is not First World. It is Third World. And there is an infinite difference.

III. Art. II, Sec. 19 of the Constitution as a Basis for the Charge of Economic Sabotage and Subversion of the Constitution.

The Constitution has a vital principle which commands that the State shall develop a self-reliant and independent national economy effectively controlled by Filipinos.

Like the directives of the Magna Carta, this is a directive which cannot be taken lightly, more so because it is a constitutional decree, and no one, riot even the President of this republic, has the right or liberty to substitute for it his or her personal economic philosophy.

But that is exactly what the technocrats of President Aquino are doing. They are pursuing an economic programme that flagrantly overrides the constitutional directive. The consequences of that programme would make us dependent on imports not only for our requirements of manufactured goods - but for our requirements of agricultural products as well.

A self-reliant economy is essentially one that produces what it needs; at least its basic needs. How can the State develop such an economy through Free Trade? How can self-reliance be fostered by a policy which deliberately overlooks the development of industries?

The whole point of economic protectionism and industrialization is precisely to force an economy towards self-reliance and independence. But those are the very objectives which the government's programme rejects.

We are in crisis because over the years the technocrats have conditioned the economy to rely on imports and loans for the nation's basic needs. We have now reached a point when we cannot even plant rice or install traffic lights without having to import or borrow and kneel before our creditors. To plant rice, we must have fertilizer. But we have not developed an adequate fertilizer industry. So we import. Importation requires dollars. And since we are constantly short of dollars, we borrow. We are constantly short of dollars because import liberalization, or what effectively amounts to free trade, has induced the economy to squander its dollars on luxuries and non-essentials instead of allocating these to essential and basic industries.

Do you realize, Mr. Secretary, that since we joined GATT in 1975, we have come to import more luxury items than we do machineries and capital goods?

IN 1975, our importation of luxury items amounted only to $210 Million, while our importation of machines amounted to $1.1 Billion. By 1987, one year after EDSA, our importation of luxuries had already reached $1.5 Billion, while our importation of machines and capital goods was at the level that it was in 1975, or $1.1 Billion.

The following figures, taken from the latest issue of the Asia Development Bank's Key Indicators of developing member countries, illustrate the criminal consequences of the import liberalization programme which started with our membership in GATT in 1975.

Luxury Imports Imports of Machineries (in Million US$)

	Luxury Imports	Imports of Machineries
1975	210	1,198
1976	316	1,162
1977	309	1,098
1978	502	1,411
1979	663	1,798
1980	922	1,958
1981	1,095	1,894
1982	1,081	1,772
1983	1,135	1,683
1984	1,475	1,129
1985	1,127	760
1986	1,232	839
1987	1,531	1,193

Consider, Mr. Secretary, the stark and dramatic contrast with South Korea.

Luxury Imports		Imports of Machineries (in Million US$)
1975	4	1,926
1976	10	2,427
1977	12	2,952
1978	9	4,996
1979	48	6,154
1980	62	5,001
1981	140	6,037
1982 .	95	6,011
1983	99	7,589
1984	106	9,817
1985	97	10,648
1986	304	10,640
1987	520	13,813
1988	152	18,242

And Estanislao and Paderanga would now reduce tariffs to an absolute maximum of 30%.

A country that is spending more on luxuries than it is on capital goods is obviously a country that is far from travelling the road towards economic self-reliance.

Compare, to stress the point, the following comparative figures as of 1987 (latest available year) which show imports by countries of luxuries as a proportion or percent of their total imports.

Country
Luxury Imports as % of total Imports

Philippines	21.3%
Thailand	2.4%
Singapore	1.6%
Malaysia	0.9%
Korea	1.3%
Indonesia	11.7%
Hong Kong	0.7%
China	0.5%
Taiwan	3.7%

I don't think there is need of further argument to show that import liberalization, as conceived and applied by the economic managers of Marcos and Aquino, constitutes high treason and subversion of our laws and the Constitution. In the fierce global economic war now raging, the technocrats have delivered this nation to its adversaries through their programme of economic disarmament, and steered the country to the road of criminal prodigality.

The nation's economic programme makes outright mockery of the constitutional directive for the state to "develop a self-reliant and independent national economy."

We don't have a national economy. The technocrats don't believe in developing a national economy. They believe in an economy dependent on foreign suppliers, on international creditors, and foreign investors. Hong Kong, which is apparently their ideal, is the exact opposite of a national economy.

It is the embodiment of a colony that has become part of the global economy, absolutely bereft of that national character and independence of which the Constitution speaks.

The Roots of Betrayal

There can be no question that Virata, Estanislao and company were, and are, conscious that their economic philosophy and the policies dictated by that philosophy, collide with and undermine the legislated and constitutionally-decreed objectives of state.

The Magna Carta was the product of a lengthy and considerably publicized parliamentary debate. It was not a document that was surreptiously made public policy the way the IMF/WB conditionalities have been made public policy. As for the constitutional mandate that the state shall develop a self-reliant and independent national economy, the economic managers, being state functionaries, are conclusively presumed to be aware of its existence.

Why then their public defiance of our laws?

How could Virata and Patemo, for example, have defied Marcos openly on the 11 major industrial projects at a time when what Marcos said, or even wished, was law, and knowing how urgently Marcos was pushing his projects through.

The answer is, that these functionaries, by and large, are backed by a powerful constituency. And that constituency is no less than the international creditors of this country, as well as the foreign governments behind those creditors. This has been an open secret all along. Marcos, the dictator, was being dictated upon by the IMF/WB, just as Cory is being so dictated now. For Marcos and Cory to defy the functionaries would be to court political disaster.

Marcos' political disaster, Mr. Secretary, actually began when he announced, and insisted on, his 11 major industrial projects. From then on, Virata, if you will recall, began to be talked about as Marcos' possible successor.

Juan T. Gatbonton, writing in the Hong Kong based magazine insioht in 1981, put it succinctly when he explained what he called the political clout of Virata and the economic managers.

Virata and the economic managers he represents have an independent constituency whose good will is more and more crucial to the regime, if it is to carry out its ambitious development plans. This constituency is made up of international lending and regulatory agencies like the World Bank and the IMF, plus multinational bankers, financiers and corporate investors.

The technocrats thus hold a potentially stronger hand in bargaining with Mr. Marcos on policy-decisions than any possible grouping of politicians can have. (insight, September 1981)

When Marcos announced his 11 major industrial projects, one of those in his cabinet who led the opposition against the projects was then Minister of Trade Luis Villafuerte. (Evening Post, Nov. 10,1979). Villafuerte had been recruited by Marcos from Bancom Development Corporation.

But the high proof dramatizing the link between the technocrats and the IMFAVB is supplied by the ease with which the former change employment loyalties on retirement from government.

Virata and Sicat, for example, are currently serving the IMFAVB as executive director and consultant, respectively. Virata is also consultant to U.S. Aid.

Vicente Valdepefias, who succeeded Sicat in NEDA, is a member of Virata's consulting group, and on retirement from government was engaged by Citibank N A. on debt rescheduling.

More recently, Ernest Leung, former finance undersecretary, joined the World Bank as executive director. Leung was the third member of the negotiating panel during the time of Ongpin and Jayme. The announcement of his appointment said that the post he would assume at the World Bank is the "highest position to be attained by a Filipino." (Daily Globe, January 23, 1990).

Estanislao is known as a ranking official of the Center for Research and Communications (CRC). That agency in turn is known to serve the consulting requirements of transnational corporations.

Vicente Jayme was recruited to government from the Philippine Development Corporation (PDCP), of which he was then president. PDCP is a major beneficiary of concessional loans extended by an affiliate of the IMFAVB, which loans are in turn re-lent to domestic companies. Much of PDCP profits are made from the spread between the interest charged PDCP by the IMFAVB and the interest charged domestic borrowers by PDCP. PDCP, in turn, eventually became a subsidiary of the Far East Bank, which Fernandez headed before he became CB Governor.

If one wonders at the ease with which the IMFAVB succeeds in having their conditionalities accepted by the government, one only has to look into the background of our economic functionaries; before they joined government, and after they had retired from government.

Patemo, for example, on retirement from the Executive branch, was conferred by the Japanese government one of the highest awards which that country could bestow on a non-Japanese national.

Armando Fabella, who, during the time of Macapagal, officially recommended that nationalism be downgraded as an element of public policy, and who, during Marcos' time, opposed the nationalist policies of then CB Governor Licaros, now reportedly serves the IMF full time on a foreign assignment. A book by American scholar, Robin Broad, recounts Fabella's role in the overhaul of the nation's financial policies along directions prescribed by the IMF. She cites Fabella, commenting on nationalist opposition within the bank, that "they do not understand that we must acknowledge the IMF and World Bank can conduct superior empirical investigations." (Broad, Unequal Alliance 143).

The facility with which Philippine debt negotiators transfer employment loyalties from the government to its international creditors has caught the attention of three senators who have introduced a bill that would ban negotiators from accepting positions with the IMFAVB and other creditor institutions.

Media report on the bill, sponsored by Senators Estrada, Romulo and Pimentel, informs us that the bill was prompted by the perception that the practice, object of the proposed prohibition, opens up possibilities of economic treason.

What is surprising is that it has taken this long for such a bill to have been conceived, and it is not even certain that it will pass. The collusion between the technocrats and the IMFAVB was common knowledge during Marcos' time and was recognized as early as then to have been the central factor behind the nation's predicament. But even the Constitutional Commission, which was largely composed of anti-Marcos personalities, did not touch on the cancer.

The roots of that cancer, Mr. Secretary, go way beyond the particular personalities we have discussed. Virata, Estanislao and company are but reflections of a higher force of which Senator Tydings, the author of the Philippine Independence Law, spoke when he testified against the infamous Bell Trade Act of 1946. That Act, if you will recall, tied promised American post-war assistance to the Philippine to two conditions: one, that we extend the free trade relation between the Philippines and the United States beyond independence; and the other, was the notorious parity amendment.

That Act was opposed by nationalists on the ground, among others, that the continuation of free trade would preserve the colonial and non-industrial character of our economy.

Speaking of the higher force behind that bill, which was represented here by the U.S. Resident Commissioner, Paul V. McNutt, Tydings said, in testimony before the American Congress:

I have no right to quote the Governor (McNutt) but I think that fundamentally he is opposed to Philippine ~ Independence, and if you would ask him he would tell you so. The truth of the matter is that most of the people, outside the Filipinos, who favor this bill are fundamentally opposed to

Philippine independence. I do not like to mention names. Their whole philosophy is to keep the Philippines economically even though we have lost them politically. (Cited in Jenkins, American Economic Policy Towards the Philippines 56).

The conditionalities which our economic functionaries have not only accepted too readily, but which they defend diligently, represent the extension of the terms of the Bell Trade Act which Recto described as reflective of America's "anti-industrialization policy in the Philippines."

They represent the conditionalities of American imperialism. In that imperialism, Mr. Secretary, lies the roots of betrayal, and of our nation's tragedy. It is an imperialism that has worked its processes into the very interstices of our socio-political and cultural life: not only in our technocracy, but in our schools, in civic organizations, in the business community, in the military and the Church.

Virata, Fernandez, Jayme, Paterno, Estanislao and company would never be tolerated in countries like Japan, South Korea, Taiwan, China and the Soviet Union, where nationalism functions as a religion. In those countries, they would be regarded as something more reprehensible than common criminals. But here, they are honored by society, and some are even sponsored by the Church for senatorial and other public positions.

Do you wonder, Mr. Secretary, why alone in Asia the Philippines remains excluded, by its own apparent choice, from the drama of human progress and liberation, as billions of Asians surface from the depths of colonial exploitation, to create a new world of their own, where hunger and deprivation will soon be unknown.

Asia today is experiencing the most significant development in its long history. It is working out, finally, its own industrial revolution; a revolution which the powers behind the IMFAVB had long suppressed. In human history, Mr. Secretary, that is the one revolution that has really counted, because it contains the essential formula against poverty and backwardness.

That is the revolution which imperialism, institutionalized in the IMF/WB, and its domestic surrogates, would deny us.

What to Do: Towards an Alternative and Emergency Programme

I realize, Mr. Secretary, that no one has a moral right to criticize a government besieged by crisis without presenting a plausible alternative, and it is that spirit that I now outline the essential elements of that alternative. I am prepared to elaborate on this on future occasions.

I. Re-establish the Foreign Exchange Control System and Effect a Dollar Saving of at Least $3 Billion a Year

The alternative programme should immediately dismantle the system which induces desperately needed dollar assets to be squandered on non-essentials. Those assets should be applied exclusively to absolute necessities. A system which allows the country to spend on luxuries more than what it invests in the machineries of production is obviously a system gone berserk. That is why import liberalization and free trade constitute high treason. In these items, and for the next five years at least, the dollars of the country should be used for the main part (1) to finance the basic industries that would enable this nation to survive, and (2) to cover importation of vital necessities indispensable to life, health and production. Outside of these, no dollar disbursements should be allowed.

Specifically, this means:

1. All importation of non-essentials shall be absolutely prohibited. Other items, already being produced locally, should be subject at least to quantitative restrictions.

   This step alone should automatically result in a dollar saving of at least $2.5 Billion a year, an amount that represents what we have to borrow regularly to maintain our economic viability.

2. A moratorium should be declared on all remittances of profitby transnational corporations and foreign investors. Foreign investments now amount to some $4 Billion. Assuming a return on these investments of 10%, this means annual earnings of $400 Million. We assume that at least 80% of that is remitted every year. That translates into $320 Million a year remittance of profits.

3. A ban on foreign travel, applicable to government officials and private citizens alike, except for absolutely necessary functions.

These three steps alone should result in dollar savings that would start us on the road to economic viability. Should the IMF reject a programme based on foreign exchange controls, then we should automatically withdraw from that organization.

II. Programme to Attract Back the $20 Billion Overseas Investment of Filipinos

Coupled with the foregoing programme of foreign exchange austerity, the country should launch a drive to attract back the billions of overseas investments made by Filipinos over the last 25 years. Those investments have been estimated to be as much as $20 Billion. A fractional success on this score, coupled with the dollar savings from the programme of dollar austerity, should enable us to live independently of our creditors. But, more than that, the programme would make us a viable proposition even for the creditors.

III. Abandon System of Floating Rate

One of the main objectives of the programme would be to remove the destabilizing elements in policy. This means:

1. Abandonment of the floating rate system, and re-adoption of the fixed rate of exchange, to be defended by the rigorous application of dollar controls.

   The floating system of exchange rate is so destabilizing that not even Hong Kong has dared adopt it.

IV. Temporary Take-over by the State of the Banking System

For the next five years, at least, the banking system should be subjected to absolute discipline because it is the principal source of capital leakage, and has functioned as a vital mechanism for wealth concentration. The emergency programme should therefore place the system under state ownership.

With the banking system under state ownership, the government can then launch a real drive to infuse money and credit in the countryside, and to finance priority industries, on the basis of low rates of interest. There is no point planning on increased productivity with interest rates as high as 28%.

Under the prevailing system, the entire economy has simply been working for the banks. This situation should be reversed. The banks should be made to work for the economy, and not the other way round. This can be accomplished only through nationalization of the banking system.

V. Restore Anti-Usury Law

The anti-usury law should be restored. Industries that have been charged usuriously by the banks should be given a moratorium on debt payments and their interest obligations adjusted.

VI. Economic Justice for Workers and Farmers

The emergency programme should then tackle the problem of the workers and farmers. Workers should be compensated for the punishment inflicted on them by the policies of the technocrats since martial law, and their demand for living wage automatically granted. Farmers, in turn, should be assured of a guaranteed market price for their produce in order to stimulate agricultural production. The current debacle of the Uruguay Round of international trade negotiations has underscored the enormous subsidies being extended by the developed countries to their respective farm sectors, and we can do no less for our farmers whose purchasing power must be guaranteed by the government if this country is to get moving.

VII. Coordinate Agrarian Reform with Countryside Industrialization

The state should proceed immediately with a coordinated programme of agrarian reform and countryside industrialization. One without the other would be ineffectual. The entire countryside developmental strategy should be overhauled with emphasis placed on the introduction of basic support services and the introduction of machine-based livelihood enterprises. The strategy adopted by the Indian government on this matter should be studied and emulated in their relevant parts.

VIII. Establish Major Industrial Projects

The emergency programme should lose no time establishing the basic heavy industries needed to enable us take off to at least emergent NIC status. Leading these would be the integrated steel, machine tool, metallurgical, engineering and fabricating industries. Marcos was on the right track with his 11 major industrial projects, and those should be implemented immediately.

IX. Automatic Reduction of Budget of Executive, Congress andthe Military by at Least 25% and Increase the Budget for Education and Science.

The Executive Department should be persuaded to reorganize and cut its budget by at least 25%, and Congress and the military should do likewise. Education and Science development, however, should, for obvious reasons, be increased by that much.

X. Compel Oil Companies to Operate at a Loss for the Next Three Years Under Pain of Confiscation

The oil companies should be asked to share the misery of the nation, and to operate, if need be, at a loss for the next three years. They have, after all, milked this country dry over the last fifty years. Should they refuse, then they should be nationalized, to be paid for in 50-year bonds with 6% interest.

The steps and policies outlined above are calculated to meet two overriding necessities of the moment. One is to put a bottomline to the crisis, and the other is to lay the foundation for the future advance of the economy.

What terrifies people about the crisis is that there appears no bottom to it. People might be able to live with P16/liter gasoline, or with a P28:$I exchange rate, but the question is, where does that spiral end? Correspondingly, this is what disheartens the people about government. Government seems absolutely bereft of any plan or strategy to establish a bottom for the crisis, much less establish the foundation for economic advance.

I realize that the package of policies I have suggested is not ideal, but those who would criticize or oppose it should present their alternative.

Central to the alternative programme I am suggesting is the assertion by the state of its sovereignty over the nation's international reserves and the domestic market. The floating rate and import liberalization are policies that require the surrender by the state of its economic sovereignty, which is what we have done, and which primarily explains the chaos that has now engulfed us.

Mr. Secretary, the crisis we face is not only a crisis of the economy. It is a crisis that involves no less than the national security, and unless a bottomline were established immediately, that crisis can only spell the literal fragmentation and disintegration of the state.

That is why it is of utmost urgency that the state now asserts its economic sovereignty.

If you have no fundamental objection to the alternative programme outlined above, then I must ask you to throw the full weight and influence of your office behind it because your office can do no less.

Eighteen years ago, when martial law was declared, the Department of Defense issued a warrant for my arrest for no crime other than the fact that I had authored a paper warning the 1971 Constitutional Convention, of which I was then a member, of the policies to which the state had been committed by the technocracts. That was then considered subversion.

I think events have vindicated my assessment of the treason behind the policies of the technocrats, and by this time your office should be sufficiently enlightened and convinced as to who the real subversives are.

If you believe in my assessment that the highest interest of this nation, including its security, have been betrayed, and are being betrayed, by the economic managers, you have no choice, Mr. Secretary, but to train your sights on them this .time. If you could find it in your heart to have caused my detention in 1972, for the things I had written, you should be able to find it in your heart to arrest the technocrats for the damage that their policies have wrought on this country.

Should the government persist on pursuing the current thrust of policy, which is so manifestly subversive of the nation's economic sovereignty and security, we might consider that the Constitution contains a sensitive principle not found in the two earlier constitutions. That principle is in Art. 11, Sec. 3 which provides that: 'The Armed Forces ofthe Philippines is to secure the sovereignty ofthe State and the integrity of the national territory."

Note that under the charter, the mission of the Armed Forces is not confined to the traditional one of defending the nation's physical territory. It has been explicitly extended to cover the sovereignty of the state. And economic sovereignty is an integral and inalienable part of sovereignty, a concept which is indivisible.

This is a provision fraught with implications, Mr. Secretary, particularly in the context of the growing nationalism in the Armed Forces and the only too transparent nature of the IMF conditionalities which our technocrats not only accept but defend and espouse; conditionalities which unequivocably collide with and undermine the nation's political, economic and even military sovereignty.

For in essence, Mr. Secretary, that is what the crisis is all about. And the question is: should, or should not, the Armed Forces of the Philippines remain indifferent to a situation where the sovereignty of the state is in clear and present danger of being lost irretrievably through a government that in effect is being run by the surrogates of intemational finance.

To save civilian government, Mr. Secretary, I urge you to apply the maximum influence of your office to persuade this government to abandon immediately the IMF conditionalities which have brought on us nothing but disaster.

Very truly yours,
ALEJANDRO LICHAUCO

oo0Ooo

3.

Sec. Ramos Open Letter-Reply To Alejandro Lichauco

By Defense Secretary Fidel V. Ramos

Dear Mr. Lichauco:

I have read your open letter entitled "The Economic Crisis and the Treason of Policy" containing your perceptions on the following concerns: (a) the nature of the country's economic crisis and the real factors behind it; Cb) the government officials responsible for the economic crisis; (c) alternative and emergency program to cope with the prevailing crisis; and (d) what the AFP and the Secretary of National Defense should do in the face of the economic crisis. I have also read your other letter which contains your reactions to my comments on your open letter as reported by the print media.

While I am not a professional economist like you, and recognizing your special expertise in this field, allow me to react to your two letters, thus:

1. In my speech at Tayug, Pangasinan, last November 11,1990, it was not my intention to use the dedication ritesand blessing of Camp Narciso R. Ramos (so-named by virtue of RA 6711 sponsored by Congressman Conrado Estrella III) as a vehicle to expound on my views on the economy nor to assess the national economic situation. For you to better comprehend my economic vision, it may be necessary that you also refer to my other speeches wherein I said that "the foundation of our vision of a highly industrialized Philippine economy should be anchored on a scientifically and technologically advanced labor force..." and that "economic justice can be best won by free men through free enterprise..." Contrary to your percep-tions, I am in favor at industrialization for the Philippines.

2. The Philippines, indeed, is in a grave economic crisis. It would be simplistic and even misleading to say, however,

that this was principally due to free trade policy and our deliberate failure to industrialize according to your formula. The crisis is also partly triggered and/or aggravated by the communist insurgency problem, the series of coup attempts initiated by rightist elements, our huge foreign debt, the impact of the Aug. 2 Iraq invasion of Kuwait and natural disasters that hit the country such as the drought last summer, the July 16 earthquake and lately typhoon "Ruping" in the Visayas and Northern Mindanao.

3. In your open letter, you pointed out "the strategic relation between national self-sufficiency, national defense and steel." Years back, this was also the thrust of the Soviet modernization program under Stalin. The operationalization of this Soviet model, which obviously was designed to sustain the Soviet military machine of the Cold War period, caused much hardship to the Soviet people, and even to others that followed this model (like what happened in India). Adoption of the Soviet Stalinist model of industrialization at this point or at arty other point in time would have exacerbated our economic problems. Should the Philippines adopt the military-industrial complex models of the superpowers or are there more appropriate realistic approaches that can do the job for the Philippines?

4. To my mind, it is incorrect to say that the present government is deliberately against industrialization and unqualifiedly in favor of free trade. It should be stressed that in the RP Medium Term Development Plan (1987-1992), it is stated that "the government shall adopt a policy of accelerating industrialization that not only benefits entrepreneurs, industrialist and investors, but also serves the interest of Filipino end-users." The plan also requires the government to provide for trade protection through the tariff system and to institute safeguards against unfair trade practices such as dumping, outright and technical smuggling, and undervaluation. This effectively refutes your view that the government is hostile towards industrialization.

5. While I agree that the Magna Carta of Social Justice and Economic Freedom was a laudable definition of national economic goals and a clear guiding light for the country, it seems that the first step towards its effective utilization has

never been taken. First of all, these policy considerations in the form of a Congressional Resolution need to be translated into specific laws and executive directives, the violation of which ought to result in appropriate sanctions and penalties. Once this is done, then that is the time the Government can prosecute their violators.

6. You recommended that the government should take over vital industries. In some Third World countries, this proposal may have intrinsic merits. However, it is shown that in many Third World democratic countries, the prevailing formula is a mixed economy which means that as a rule, the free market economy is practiced side by side with limited state capitalism. This principle has been proven to be sound and workable in many countries. At present, the Philippines has a mixed economy and it may be disastrous if the government nationalizes vital industries just for the sake of nationalizing. The 1987 Constitution calls for Filipinization and not nationalization of our industries.

7. You contend that our past and present economic planners are guilty of treason and economic sabotage. You, certainly, are entitled to your own personal opinion. I will not comment on your accusations since the proper venue to discuss and ventilate the matter is with competent bodies like the Department of Justice and the courts. At this time, however, I strongly feel that there is no sense in fault-finding and apportioning blame. What we need to do, in my opinion, is to deal with our economic crisis pragmatically and on the basis of agreed objectives and priorities and a unified strategy - keeping in mind that the linkages of the international economic system have become so strong as to force wide-open even the most tightly controlled economics, and that our country must exploit its comparative advantage in many sectors.

In your letter you asserted that: The Secretary would make it appear that I was asking for arrests, martial law style. I never ever hinted at that, and the good Secretary should know that the country doesn't have to plunge into martial law again to arrest subversives of the type of Estanislao and company, any more than martial law is needed to arrest the nation's illegal loggers and smugglers, military rebels and leftists insurgents."

While I respect your views, I deplore your resort to generalized conclusions as to the "subversive" conduct of others who do not subscribe to your views. To prosecute Secretary Estanislao and other present and past economic planners for economic subversion would require not only the translation of the Magna Carta congressional resolution into a specific legal enactment; Are you ready or willing to substantiate your charges in a court of la w assuming there is such a law that has been violated? Our present democratic system defined by the 1987 Constitution, which I have sought to protect as a responsible official and as a concerned citizen like you, does not permit the strong armed methods that you suggest I take against your fellow economists.

To prosecute illegal loggers, smugglers, etc. is easily done, and indeed is being done, as there are already appropriate laws enacted and all that is needed is to come up with prima facie evidence, good prosecutors and upright judges. Your analogy in this instance is therefore considered just too far-fetched.

The clash of economic philosophies - say, between those who are protectionists and those who wish an open economy or a mixed economy is, I suppose, inevitable. 1 therefore suggest that there be a debate among you - the economic experts who share differing views. For this, I am available to serve as moderator and referee in an open forum - not in the boxing arena as wrongly reported by Mr. Francisco Nemenzo.

We in the Department of National Defense (1)ND) are keenly aware, perhaps more than others, of the mandate given the DND under the Constitution and existing laws. I wish to assure you that we will continue to fulfill such mandate to the best of our abilities upholding at all times the supremacy of the civilian authority. 1 am sure you will agree with me that had the DND-AFP not moved responsively in the recent past to repel and defeat the armed threats against the Republic, we would be back to martial rule that you and I and the vast majority of our people threw out at EDSA in February 1986.

With best wishes,
Very sincerely yours,
FIDEL V. RAMOS, Secretary

4.

Lichauco Open Reply to Defense Secretary Fidel V. Ramos

by Alejandro Lichauco

Dear Secretary Ramos:

I would have ignored your answer but for the ill-concealed attempt to smear me as a "Stalinist" bent on "strong armed methods" against fellow economists.

If the line of development I espouse is "Stalinist" then the term similarly applies to Recto, Nehru, Nasser, Suharto and Mahathir, all of whom saw the strategic linkage between steel and the basic industries, on one hand, and national security and defense, on the other.

Your line is old CIA hat, Mr. Secretary, which the Agency applied to Recto and Nehru during the Fifties, and you could have been more imaginative.

India, which you cite as a deplorable case of "Stalinism"*, is now a formidable industrial-military power and a democracy at the same time, able to produce her own missiles, nuclear plant, machine tools, locomotives, industrial machinery and armaments while we can't even produce a barrio-to-barrio missile.

You claim that you are also for the country's industrialization, but what industrialization do you envision? An industrialization obviously based on cottage and small-time industries.

The fact is that you echo the line of the technocrats graduated from the Center for Research and Communications and the UP School of Economics, institutions which are the ideological extensions of the IMF and the World Bank.

Instead of rising instinctively to the defense of Estanislao and company, you could have referred my letter to the Department of Justice inasmuch as I had cited specific statutory and constitutional provisions which, only too clearly, are being undermined by the IMF-dictated policies readily adopted by the technocrats. Revealingly, you claim that you, too, are for free enterprise and that you believe, to quote you, "economic justice can be best won by free men through free enterprise."

But don't you realize that free enterprise was precisely repudiated by House Joint Resolution No. 2 (Magna Carta)?

Let me quote the speech sponsoring that document, which was delivered by no less than the Speaker Jose B. Laurel, Jr.:

To achieve these objectives, it is necessary that our economy be effectively planned. Hence, the Joint Resolution provides for a "national economic development authority with powers to plan and coordinate the nation's economic activities.

This concept, I must state candidly, is at variance with free enterprise as a doctrine of development. It was the unanimous feeling of the Committee that free enterprise operates to accentuate and aggravate the gap between the rich and the poor. It also leads to a situation of wasteful competition, the uneconomic duplication of economic activities and the channeling of scarce resources to economic activities of low social rate of return.

What further evidence does one need to conclude that a specific congressional resolution, with the force of law, has been undermined by the nation's technocracy all this time, and that the IMFAVB economic philosophy, which underlies the conditionalities, squarely collides with the economic philosophy established by Congress in 1969. It was precisely against the free enterprise and free trade doctrines of the IMFAVB that the Magna Carta was directed.

If you feel that implementing legislation is necessary to authorize the arrest of the economic managers, then I suggest that your department lose no time drafting the proposed legislation for submission to Congress, and I shall only be too happy to assist you in that effort. We might even testify together on the need for such a legislation in the interest of national security.

You need not have lectured me on constitutionalism and the distastefulness of the strong armed methods associated with the dictatorship. I defied martial law from beginning to end while you supported it for 14 years.

My letter raised an important issue, and that concerned the legal as well as ethical propriety of the practice under which the nation's economic functionaries switch employment loyalties to the IMFAVB after committing the government to the onerous and one-sided conditionalities of those two institutions. Your answer is silent on that issue. Do I take it that you find nothing wrong in the behavior of Philippine debt negotiators who join the IMFAVB after yielding only too easily and readily to the dictates of those institutions while representing our government?

You dismiss as "simplistic" the view which attributes the economic crisis primarily to the free trade doctrine with which we have been forced to live under Philippine-American special relations. If so, what would be a "non-simplistic" explanation for the crisis? You cite factors such as the communist insurgency, the numerous attempts at a coup, natural disasters and Iraq's invasion of Kuwait. Are you saying that without these factors we wouldn't be in crisis? Hasn't this nation been plagued by mass poverty even before the Satur Ocampos and the Gringo Honasans appeared on the scene?

How about American imperialism? Don't you think that is a factor in our crisis?

You see, Mr. Secretary, the situation is prodding our people to search for the real causes behind the crisis, and there is a growing awareness that the usual reasons given for it, such as graft and corruption, cronyism, monopolies and over-population, don't really touch the heart of the problem. As our people witness the dramatic rise to opulence of nations once as backward and impoverished as we are, and which continue to be afflicted with the same vices that grip us, the usual explanations for our predicament simply fade away. We are not the only corrupt society in Asia, nor do we command a monopoly of favored cronies and of human fertility. So there must be a more fundamental explanation for the persistence of poverty and underdevelopment. And that is to be found, as nationalists maintain, in the self-destructive nature of our policies which, in turn, are a function of the double allegiance of the nation's leaders, particularly those who design the nation's vital policies. Those policies obviously aren't meant for our interest, but for the interest of others, and have been engineered by local functionaries with one eye to what would please and accommodate either actual or prospective principals abroad.

Civilian authorities can no longer remain unconcerned with the problem of double allegiance, particularly on the part of officials responsible for the nation's development programs and who conduct its international negotiations. You must have noticed the increasing cynicism and indignation of the public towards the way that negotiations are being conducted, and policies being conceived, by officials who eventually stray into the payroll of the nation's creditors, or who are regarded to have financial links with transnational interests.

As I pointed out in my letter, there is a provision in the Constitution which entrusts to the Armed Forces the task of securing the sovereignty ofthe state. This provision, contained in Art. 11, Sec. 3, would seem to authorize the intervention of the military in cases where the sovereignty of the state is placed in jeopardy by civilian government. This is a provision which nationalist elements in the military could possibly invoke as a reason for taking over government if the civilian authorities continue to display a wanton disregard of the nation's sovereignty in their dealings with external powers. In such a case, the military would have plausible reasons for intervening because the survival of the state, after all, is a far more important matter than the principle of civilian supremacy. What Art. 11, Sec. 3 has done is to provide the ultimate safeguard against the possible treason of civilian government.

The reason for the provision is understandable. The present constitution was drafted by persons who by and large were intensely politicized by martial law, and who saw that government, during that period, functioned mainly as a surrogate of Washington and the IMFAVB complex. In that situation, only the AFP could possibly have extricated the nation by toppling Marcos, that is, had it been imbued with a nationalist consciousness and more importantly had it been armed with a specific constitutional function to protect the sovereignty of the state.

But under the two earlier constitutions, the AFP was given no such mission. Its duty was simply to obey its commander-in-chief, even if that obedience entailed complicity in treason.

It was obviously to rectify that flaw that the article in question was conceived: to make sure that the AFP never again follow civilian authority blindly where that authority takes to the path of treason by jeopardizing either the sovereignty of the state or the integrity of its territory.

Under the present Constitution, therefore, civilian authority would be courting the intervention of the military if it continues with a national program that compromises the political integrity of the Philippines as a sovereign nation-state. That was the reason why I appealed to you to persuade this government, of which you are an important part, to abandon an economic program that so transparently undermines the economic independence of this country. As the erosion of the nation's independence, and the violation of its sovereignty, become increasingly evident, and flagrant, the government increasingly risks the intervention of a growingly nationalistic military establishment.

I made those observations in my letter as one anxious to see the supremacy of civilian government justifiably preserved. Your answer, however, has merely reinforced the impression that the high functionaries of this administration are, to say the least, hopelessly indifferent to the question of sovereignty.

Mr, Secretary, under earlier constitutions, civilian governments might have bartered the nation's sovereignty with impunity. But they can do so now only at their peril.

Very Sincerely.
ALEJANDRO LICHAUCO

ooOOoo

5.

Complaining to God Almighty

Larry Henares

First it is the corrosive lay of the land, then the utter corruption of the state of inner being:

(1)   The internet is suddenly unavailable to me, the intermittent buffering, the sudden stops in reception, the fact that I pay 12 times as much for one 10th the speed of service that Singapore gives its netizens, being charged for every minute and every fraction thereof, instead of every 3-second pulse, as in every civilized country. Fie on the National Telecommunications Commission and the Internet Exchange monopoly of Smart Communications!

(2)   My email account of larryh@mydestiny.com suddenly collapsed, expunged by experts from my computer several times but crops up every day to deny me access to my new account of hilarion.henares@gmail.com. I can't receive or send emails.

(3)   The weather sucks, heat alternates with wetness, and when the raindrops fall and instantly vaporize on the hot pavement, a swirl of germ laden dust rise to cause instant allergies and sudden colds. The torrent of rain suggests not only the weeping of angels, but also St. Peter and Paul pissing on us. On top of that the typhoons, the floods and the traffic.

(4)   Suddenly I am old, the knees go first. When I sit on a lounge chair or a Porsche car seat, it takes two men to raise me to my feet. I build my chairs and bed more than 10 inches higher so I fall on my feet instead of rise from my knees. I cannot walk without using a cane to keep my balance.

(5)   Acid reflux keeps me coughing up sticky spittle phlem, till I feel like The Blob. I am a river of piss, taking a leak every hour, and I still leak after the final shakeout. I shit in small installments four times a day. I am a total wreck.

(6)   Not really a total wreck. Vicki Belo gives me a shot of stem cells, and that makes me like Tarzan. I enjoy

myself three times a week and twice each time. I write ten broadcast articles every day. I watch half a season of TV serials daily, I take my domestic staff to movies 4 times a week. My children take me to eat out all the time, and my weight ballooned to 183 pounds. I am a very tired Superman.

(7)   I am already 91 years old, very close to the end of my life. I turn on the TV and read the newspapers on the political, social and economic situation in my country, and at the end of the day before I sleep and encounter the usual nightmares, a wave of sadness sweeps over me. ***

It is a kind of sadness that different from any other I have ever experienced, something approaching the Korean concept of Han, a complex intermingling of historical, collective and personal sorrow, an acceptance of a bitter present and a hope of a better future, with suggestions of resentment and a sense of unresolved vengeance.

Probably the most well known reference to it is the episode of season 5 of The West Wing entitled 'Han'. It describes the plight of a North Korean pianist who is asked not to defect (which he wanted to do) in order to preserve the hopes of nuclear non-proliferation talks between the USA and North Korea. What is the sorrow of one man compared to possibility of world peace among nations? President Bartlett (Martin Sheen) describes it thus: "Han, there is no literal English translation. It's a state of mind. Of soul, really. A sadness. A sadness so deep no tears will come. And yet still there's hope."

Han is passive. It yearns for vengeance, but does not seek it. Han is hoping and patient but never aggressive. It becomes part of the blood and breath of a person. There is a sense of lamentation and even of reproach toward the destiny that led to such misery.

ooo0ooo

6.

Criminals at Nine Years Old?

Father Shay Cullen
26 January 2017

Andres is just one10-year old child and he has lived on the streets of Metro Manila most of his life like thousands of other street children. They are abandoned, work as scavengers, market boys or girls and are vulnerable to sexual and physical abuse by adults. They are uneducated and without family or social welfare, care and protection. They are completely vulnerable to the influence of those who can give them food or money.

Andres was a survivor. He worked as a scavenger collecting plastic bottles and other junks to sell in order to buy enough food for the day but it was never enough. He only knew he had to get food and anything he did to survive was the right thing for him to do. He didn't get enough scraps one day and he saw a cell phone on a vendor's tray at the market and he took it. He sold it and bought food. Andres like most children didn't know if it was right or wrong. The moral or legal issue was not a reality for him. He was just hungry. He was arrested by the barangay tanod and charged with theft. Was he a criminal?

There is a majority of Filipinos who say, "No he is not." The Philippine Congress on two previous occasions said he is not. There are now voices of the police and local district officials who blame the children as young as nine years of age as notorious criminals and they say the children should be treated as criminals. They are persuading congressional representatives to amend the law and to lower the minimum age of criminal liability of the Filipino children from 15 years of age to nine years of age. They think that the child is allowed to go without any intervention to help them know right from wrong. The law directs that there be help given and intervention for children in conflict with the law. This lowering of the age of criminal liability is detrimental to children it should not be changed.

The child shall be subjected to a community-based intervention program supervised by the local social welfare and development officer, unless the best interest of the child requires the referral of the child to a youth care facility or 'Bahay Pag-asa' managed by LGUs or licensed and/or accredited NGOs monitored by the DSWD.

The law and millions of Filipinos and around the world say, "No, Andres and thousands like him are not criminals and must be helped." They and wise legislators believe that the survival of life is the greatest human need and hunger must be satisfied. Besides the Philippine law RA 9344 is benign, compassionate and enlightened and it takes into consideration that a child, especially under the age of 15, that has little schooling, lives on the streets and is always hungry cannot be held liable for adult acts that are considered adult crime.

The fact that police are complaining that criminal gangs are taking advantage of children because they cannot be held liable for crimes claim that the children work as drug couriers and should be treated as criminals and the law be changed so nine year olds can be arrested. The supporters of such a position should present solid research showing substantial figures of children being used in this way. But even if it were so then the child would not understand that he or she was doing something wrong. The power and influence of an adult in ascendency over the child is very strong. The child cannot act with free will and full knowledge and without that there is no crime. They have been coerced.

The adult drug traffickers are the criminals, not the small children. The children are innocent victims of abuse by the adults. The adult suspects ought to be arrested and charged with child abuse. The testimony of the child will be sufficient to convict the adult criminal using the child. The child can be taken into care and protection and the law provides for that intervention. In a court ruling applying the RA 9344 the judge had the following to say.

"R.A. No. 10630 addresses the concerns and criticisms of the law by amending certain provisions of R.A. No. 9344. One amendment introduced by R.A. No. 10630 is the imposition of the maximum period prescribed by law for the crime committed on any person, who in the commission of a crime, makes use, takes advantage of, or profits from the use of children, including any person who abuses his/her authority over the child or who, with abuse of confidence, takes advantage of the vulnerabilities of the child and shall induce, threaten or instigate the commission of the crime."

That is putting the burden on law enforcers to apprehend and charge the adults who use children and instigate and teach them to participate in illegal actions. The tabloid media has constantly played up the plight of the street children who have to survive alone or in groups. They present them as animal-like criminals and sometimes demonize the children.

But the desperate hungry and abandoned children are trying to meet their human needs to survive in a cruel neglectful society around them. They have been neglected, abused oppressed and jailed. Some of the Bahay Pag-asa youth centers are in fact jails in most respects and the children are in fact being punished. They provide little or no education or assistance to give the children no chance at a better life. Soon the cells will fill-up with nine year olds and suffer physical and sexual abuse in the jails if the law is changed.

What an added disgrace to the Philippines to criminalize the innocent children. Remembering the words of Jesus of Nazareth when asked who was the most important in the world. He placed a child before the crowd and said "The greatest in the Kingdom of Heaven is the one who humbles himself and becomes like this child. Whoever welcomes one such child as this welcomes me." (Matt.18; 3 -5) These are somber thoughts for those who would treat the child as a criminal at nine years old. Let your opposition be known by the chairperson of the Congressional Committee on Justice Rep. Reynaldo Umali through his Twitter account https://twitter.com/reyumali

Contact the author at:
shaycullen@preda.org

oo0Ooo

7.

No Need for Martial Law in our Police State

Rene Sagisag
Dateline, Jan 18, 2017 at Yahoo Account
<ravslaw@gmail.com>

Why should Prez Digong formally inflict martial law with its downside? It would be admitting that, at variance with his campaign promise, qua candidate, six months would not suffice to bring us to paradise. He now has an elastic, sliding scale timetable. First an extension of three months, then six, then his entire term, maybe even beyond, as Premier, to solve certain permanent problems of the human race, like graft.

Seizure of drugs worth billions? In whose possession have they been all the time in the first place?

Anyway we have had a de facto Police State since June 30, 2016. Even a cop, SPO3 Ricky Sta. Isabel - a person of interest - preferred to surrender to the NBI, not the PNP, fearing for his safety, which the terrifying scofflaw organization cannot guarantee.

Its Operation Tokhang is one manifestation of blatant human and constitutional rights abuse. The flagship is inquisitorial and represents the best thinking of centuries back. Not even Marcos, the criminal genius, had thought of anything Tokhang-like, correctly declared by the Senate as illegal, as I understand it. It openly violates R.A. No. 7438, which says the police may not even "invite" anyone, and trivializes the right to privacy, to be let and left alone. We in the Senate, in approving Sen. Bobby Tanada's laudable bill, knew how coercive and intimidating a police invite, which cannot be refused. One's right not to speak is not honored and there's always some under-the-mango-tree shyster to allow his name to be misused as one lawyer provided by the cops.

Speaker Bebot Alvarez need not name and shame anyone but urge that charges be filed, in the proper forum, not in the media. Trial and conviction by publicity is a No-No.

Digong and his puppet House - an echo, not a voice - will bring back the death penalty, by public hanging at that, to reduce the numbers of the poor. The elite honored in some necktie party? They pass the laws, which represent their biases. But, there may be hope in the Senate, where I once led the opposition to the anti-poor measure (1987-92).

Sen. Manny Pacquiao, said to owe the BIR billions, wouldn't be touched for that of course and Digong even touts him to be his successor. The BIR announced no-more-shame-campaign, a practice I had disagreed with for decades, beginning with Mayor Lim's spray-paint campaign against druggies. Therefore, the BIR would not issue posters announcing that Manny seems to be our Top Tax Evader, in the billions.

And Untouchable Manny, the third man in the aborted Fighting Trillanes versus Flash Zubiri bout last Tuesday, is said to be juggling his sked to have four(!) bouts this year. One problem is who he will fight and where. He has to accept that he no longer sells as before and he needs time to study and train to run a country of maybe 120M rabbits in the next decade. He faces at least 30 suits in the U.S. for misrepresentation, for reportedly concealing an injured shoulder. Can he update us on these lawsuits before juries that can ran away?

And what about his inviting Bato and family to Nevada to watch him fight at his expense? Illegal and unethical, arguably, which appears not to bother the Senate, he being a formidable Digong Sipsip. Take that, Leila! (Canada' s premier is facing an inquiry for having accepted a family vacation invite to the Caribbean.)

But, maybe Prez Manny won't have as bloody a first semester as we have just seen. And amateurish, even childish, in some ways. Rookie misjudgments of which we hope to have fewer in this, the second semester, as the Administration leaves Kindergarten.

It is all right to improve ties with Russia and China but why needlessly offend the U.S., the U.N., Australia, and the European Union?

What programs does Digong have to improve working conditions in government, not only of cops (and soldiers)? Not martial law.

But, clarity we need. The Secretary of Clarification, Retraction, Apology and Pi's (SCRAP) had better improve, such as dealing with Digong's recorded statement that me might inflict martial law, in language eerily reminiscent of Macoy, "to save the Republic." Utterly lame and confusing statements by the Cabinet on what was said by a Prez seemingly inarticulate and unable to express himself clearly.

A recent Times editorial quoted Angie Dickinson as saying, "You know my story. I am pretty." And everybody knew her story. (Her legs were insured with Lloyds, for $1M!) I was a young law teacher when she was the talk of the town, along with our Divina Valencia. (Vivian Velez came a decade later.)

But, what if a Mae West-type asks Digong and chum Mon Tulfo: "Are those guns in your pockets? Or are you just glad to see me?"

We need clearer communication skills, in very short supply in the Palace in the last six months. There are many grammar schools nearby. One is St. Jude. But, the way Digong & Co. at times talk makes us feel we need to learn Chinese. Or Greek. It may be in the Tower of Babel in the Palace that we may need Zipper Lane. Ang dadaldal; wala namang pong katuturan madalas.

Some serious study is required in dealing with the 5/6 phenomenon, of losing certain benefits from the European Union if we keep reducing our population problem with EJKs, etc. (we now plead for help in setting up rehab centers, which should have been built much earlier, before the bloody spree).

We are glad not to hear of Digong jet-skiing in the West Philippine Sea. We don't want him drowning. But, DFA Sec. Jun Yasay had to do a better job in explaining why we allow China to enter our home and screw the kasambahay, a daughter and the wifey, and announce big economic benefits coming our way. One perception of it is that we are now engaged in high-class prostitution. Would we really do anything for money?

No respect for human rights. None for human dignity.

What happens to national honor, pride and sovereignty?

Good to read that the Prez met the new American Ambassador, of South Korean descent, without Digong telling him what our Numero Uno thought of him and his mother, and where to go, the unfortunate fate of an American Prez of African descent.

We want to see a vigorous anti-corruption program, which should not focus on prosecution alone, but on improving working conditions, better pay, health care and pension programs (not only for cops [and soldiers]), the non-rocket-science secret of others.

No, Sir, you used to be Mayor, but now you are our Prez, by the grace of Providence and our people. Time to think national even international, not parochial.

No need to make us pee in our pants. Stop campaigning, start governing.

You may start by marrying Honeylet - your partner, significant other, companion, mistress, kulasisi, or "concubine, " in a sense - and stop showing that you are above the laws of God and Man. God's time has come, to avoid awkwardness, if only in official receptions.

You are a Role Model.

We look around and see split-level Christianity all around.

Or be reminded of what Chesterton observed, It has neither succeeded nor failed simply because It has never been tried.

Saguisag & Associates Lawyers
4045 Bigasan Street, Palanan, 1235 Makati
Office Nos. (+632) 551-6350

ooo0ooo

8.

On the issue of VP Robredo and the Vin d'honneur

Felipe Q. Buencamino
Dateline, January 16, 2017

Vice-President Leni Robredo's office: "Our office received an invitation to the Vin d'honneur via e-mail last Dec. 28, 2016. On Jan. 4, Malacañang called the Office to retract the invitation, stating that the guest list was limited."

Presidential spokesman Ernesto Abella: "It is the prerogative of the Palace to invite those who they feel is needed to be there."

So the Palace did not feel the Vice-President needed to be at the Vin d'Honneur?

What is this Vin d'Honneur thing anyway? It is an official function hosted by the president as head of state, a tradition that goes back decades.

To quote an article titled "Briefer on the New Year Vin d'Honneur 2013," from the government's Official Gazette:

"In times past, the annual New Year's reception was quite the social event, the traditional "open house" being an opportunity for high government officials, former presidential families, members of Congress, the Judiciary, the diplomatic corps, and business and social circles to mingle freely and relatively informally in the Palace.

"After the EDSA Revolution, the traditional New Year's reception was continued, but came to be known from the administration of President Corazon C. Aquino onward, as a Vin d'honneur. The term comes from the French practice, which means 'wine of honor.' It traditionally takes place at the end of inaugurations, speeches, and ceremonies that marks the social life of the French provinces. In the Philippine context, over the years it has come to be considered primarily a diplomatic event, which features a toast exchanged between the President of the Philippines and the Papal Nuncio, who is the Dean of the Diplomatic Corps."

(To read the full version of the Vin d'Honneur briefer on the Official Gazette Web site, please visit the link,

http://bit.ly/wineofhonor)

What is the Vice-President? Under the Constitution, the only function of the Vice-President is to wait for the presidency to be vacated.

But because no one knows if and when the Presidency will be vacated, it is vital that his successor hit the ground running should the unthinkable happen.

That's why, friend or foe, the President must keep the Vice-President in the loop as far as matters of state are concerned.

And that includes giving the rest of the world, the local officialdom, and his potential successor an opportunity to get to know each other. Official state functions are one of those getting to know occasions.

The problem with Rodrigo Duterte and his administration of former classmates, former dormmates, frat *brods*, *kababayans*, and buddies is that they are unable to differentiate between the person and the office.

They see nothing wrong with Duterte cursing and insulting foreign leaders or just anyone he wants to when he feels like it. They see no difference between Duterte the President of the Philippines and Duterte as Digong. "He's just being real" is the popular refrain.

But there is a difference. A crucial difference. When one speaks as President of the Philippines, he speaks for the entire nation and when he speaks as Digong he only speaks for himself. He can say anything he wants in private but a certain decorum is expected of him in public because he represents, is in fact the personification of the entire nation.

The same thing applies to not inviting the Vice-President to official state functions. It is not just Leni that the Palace downgraded, it is the Vice-Presidency as well.

The Constitution created the Vice-President for a reason, and only an idiot will not see the wisdom behind creating a position that will enable a smooth transition of power should the unthinkable happen.

It is okay to mount a propaganda campaign against Leni the politician and to destroy her chances of ever holding any sort of elected office again because that's politics. But it is not okay to downgrade the position of Vice-President as needless because that position should be beyond politics.

There are times when our people and the world must be reminded that when matters of state are involved we are above petty political squabbles. And that's why the Vice-President should always be in official state functions.

Felipe Q. Buencamino is a senior fellow of Action for Economic Reforms
www.aer.ph

oo0Ooo

9.

On the Death of JOSE RIZAL and the Retraction Lies, Scandal, and Deceptions

Poch Suzara
Dateline, December 11, 2009

OUR ASIAN NEIGHBORS

The secret why other Asian neighbors are economically ahead of the Philippines is no secret at all. They have been substantiating to the fullest extent possible what Jose Rizal, our nation's chief hero, was precisely saying to fellow Filipinos more than a hundred years ago: Wake up! Embrace science! Utilize the scientific way of thinking! Start to emulate the freethinkers! Knowledge is the heritage of mankind, but only the courageous inherit it! We can only serve our country by telling the naked truth. However bitter it may be.

Indeed, as the only Catholic country in Asia, we would rather have more faith in prayer and theology than take advantage of the power of knowledge, science, and technology.

RIZAL'S RETRACTION SCANDAL

If Rizal had retracted from his attacks against the teachings and practices of the Catholic Church, and if, according to his Catholic biographer Leon M. Guerrero, Rizal had gone to confession four times, heard mass in his death-cell, and received holy communion before he was executed, then Rizal should be branded a traitor to all freedom fighters. He deserved not to be respected or admired as a hero. He should, instead, be canonized a saint of God. But then again, if Rizal had retracted, why then should the church feel dedicated to get Rizal's true character expunged out of the Filipino psyche? The truth of the matter was that the Church did everything possible to counteract Rizal's honest-to-goodness scientific temper of mind. Indeed, in his Noli and Fili, Rizal exposed the Philippine damaged culture caused by organized superstition otherwise popularly known as Christianity. Thus, the story of his retraction was nothing more than a theological concoction to sanitize, if not to neutralize considerably the volume of Rizal's humanistic and scientific messages to the Filipino as a people.

RIZAL'S BIOGRAPHER

Rizal's biographer, Leon M. Guerrero, clearly notes that Rizal returned to the Church of his youth in extremes of self-abasement, frenziedly in childlike fashion, spending the remaining hours of earning indulgences from purgatory by confessing four times, and obsequiously attending to Fr. Balaguer and Villaclara's wishes. In brief, according to this biographer, Rizal died as a timid coward. Indeed, according to this official government commissioned biographer, our national hero in the end turned out to be a turncoat, a creepy-crawly coward.

But then again, four years before his death, Rizal in 1882 wrote a letter to Gregorio Aglipay: It is probable that I will be executed, then they will try to bring along my moral death by covering my memory with slander.

THE SHAME IN RIZAL'S LIFE AND TIMES

The shame in Rizal's life is not the retraction of his deeds, writings or personal conduct. Such retraction was only a frailocratic figment of the impoverished priestly imagination. The real shame comes from the Filipino historians and other Catholic writers, not to mention the Knights of Rizal themselves who believed not in Rizal's power of intellect, but believed instead his enemies, the friars, who invented sacred lies about this great man. Via the control of the system of education in the Philippines , these friars have and still are blocking, expediently and consistently, Rizal's qualified and legitimate entry into the world stage as one of mankind's greatest thinkers. But then again how can the world learn of Rizal's intellectual power if the Filipinos themselves know so little of the health and wealth of this great 19th century Filipino scientists, humanist, thinker, and writer?

SANTO THOMAS UNIVERSITY AND ATENEO

Rizal was a product of Ateneo and Santo Thomas; yet both Catholic universities continue to assassinate the character of this great humanist thinker. Rizal had learned on his own initiative, outside academic wall, how to think deeply and how to embrace intellectual honesty valiantly. Indeed, to this day, all Catholic universities still teach that during his last day on this earth, just hours before he was executed for his principles, noble values, and rational beliefs, Rizal retracted and went back to embrace the Catholic Church and its teachings. What brazen lies! It is no less than a tall story. A cheap shot at a great man. Otherwise, after his death, he should have been given a Catholic burial and his bodily remains not just put inside an old sack and thrown in the Paco Cemetery in the corner where heretics are stashed away like dead animals.

RIZAL AND EDUCATION

Jose Rizal pointed out that evolution in education, (not reliance on foreign investments), is the best hope of the nation to enjoy the highest standard of living and thinking. The system of education for the Filipino must be based on science and technology, and not on prayers and theology. Indeed, according to Rizal, a free nation can rise no higher than the standard of beliefs and values set in its schools, colleges, and universities. In there hope for the Philippines? Yes, there is! But first its system of education must be radically revamped. No more silly prayers to support a stupid theology. Only more science and more technology via more scientific method of thinking.

RIZAL - THE HUMANIST

Rizal struggled not only against Spanish authority, but against superstition. He fought not in the battlefield, but in the minds of men and in the hearts of women. Rizal was Asia's first scientific-humanist thinker put to death a century ago by musketry as authorized by theocracy. The same Catholic theocracy today that is keeping the Filipino youth via education to live in guilt and to fear new and fresh ideas; indeed, to keep away from the free market of ideas, and to hate, at the same time, the freethinkers, especially the books written by freethinkers. Blotting out their brains, Rizal wrote, in faith, prayers, masses, novenas, superimposed these onto native superstition.

A CENTURY AFTER RIZAL'S DEATH

After a hundred years, how influential has Jose Rizal been on the Filipino as a people? Millions today would readily give credence by listening to the words of a Mike Velarde of El Shaddai preaching pastoral nonsense derived from the bible, a book written not by Filipinos but by foreigners. Only a handful of scholars would care to read and understand the real Rizal and carry out his principles and ideals for the achievement of pride, dignity, intellectual and scientific honesty for the Filipino as a nation. And to think, the Jews, the Chosen People of God, never considered the bible as a holy book at any time in their history. In fact, the Jews live in a Jewish State. They do not live in a Christian country, the land where Jesus Christ was presumed born.

JOSE RIZAL AND NINOY AQUINO

Ninoy Aquino said: The Filipino is worth dying for. Well, Ninoy is a hero today. Filipinos killed him. Imagine Jose Rizal having said too: The Catholics are worth dying for. Rizal today would be a saint. The Catholics had him killed. And this is exactly how sick we all are today as the Sick Man of Asia. Thanks to Filipino catholic theologians, like Father Jose S. Arcilla, S.J., and his gang who have not ceased writing brazen lies about Jose Rizal's soul saved in heaven. What a crock of religious hypocrisy!

RIZAL - THE GREATEST OF FILIPINO THINKERS

Rizal, indeed, was a great thinker. He clearly saw in his day what we vaguely see around us today: religion and diseases flourishing hand in hand under ignorance, filth, hate, and poverty. What irked the friars against Rizal was his refusal to continue to believe in Christianity; for, he learned to be on the side of humanity. For my part, if there's life after death, it's great thinkers like Rizal that I should wish to be with. Otherwise, if I will just find myself in the company of Filipino theologians, or among the Opus Dei gang, the kind of people who had Rizal put to death, please Lord spare me the sacred horror. I would rather be forever in hell.

THE SPANISH FRIARS
If the Spanish friars had only introduced the concept of humanism instead of establishing in the Philippines religious barbarism and other forms of supernaturalism, Filipino priests like Gomez, Burgos, and Zamora need not have been garroted to death for wanting reforms within the Catholic Church in their time. Moreover, great thinkers like Jose Rizal need not have been executed by firing squad for writing to promote common human decency amongst Filipino to learn to enjoy throughout the land national pride and Asian dignity.

LIES AND DECEPTION ABOUT JOSE RIZAL
Rizal never said or wrote: It was my pride that ruined me. Those words were put into the mouth of Rizal by his official prize-winning biographer Leon Maria Guerrero who believed, as a Catholic, the Rizal retraction story as concocted by the sciolistic friars. Moreover, Rizal never got rid of his political appetite, moral perplexities, and intellectual pride. On the contrary, Rizal chose to die proudly. After the superstitious friars stripped him of his dignity, it was no longer possible for Rizal to go on living as a decent man and as a thinking Filipino.

RIZAL'S UNFINISHED REVOLUTION
Rizal called for the revolution of the mind to throw off the exploitation of man by man under the inspiration of superstition. This was a century ago. But due to our fear of the Lord and our love for that pie in the sky, Rizal's call for that revolution of the human intellect ended up to what is recognized today in the history of the Filipino people as the unfinished revolution. Rizal wrote: I am not writing for this generation, but for those yet to come. If this one could read what I have written, it would burn my books, my whole life's work. But the generation that deciphers these characters will be a learned generation; it will understand me and say: Not everyone slept during the night of our forefathers! These strange characters, the sense of

mystery they will create, will save my work from the ignorance of men, just as strange rites and the sense of the unknown have preserved many truths at the hands of priests.

RIZAL'S KILLERS

What kind of men needed to see Rizal dead, discarded and forgotten? Were they men of reason, logic, science or philosophy? Were they avid readers, critical thinkers, or scientific investigators? Were they men at home with civilized humanity? No! On the contrary, Rizal's enemies were the friends of blind faith: - the superstitious primitives, the sanctimonious hypocrites, and those indeed who were selfish, greedy, corrupt, stupid, and insane. Rizal's enemies of a hundred years ago, are still the same enemies we have today. They are the ones insisting that it makes no difference whether Rizal retracted from his religious, political and philosophical principles or not. What a silly conclusion to bestow upon the greatest of Filipino seminal thinker who died for the liberation of the Filipino mind and heart, and indeed, for all mankind. Shame on you cowards - you so-called Knights of Rizal.

WHAT IS A GREAT FILIPINO

A great Filipino is one who has had the intellect and the courage to put more sense where the theologians and the politicians in cahoots together have put only nonsense making for our sick society. In the 500 years of Christianity in the Philippines, only one rare Filipino had the courage and the intellect to stand up against great odds to be a great Filipino - Jose Rizal - a truth-seeker, a scientist, and a humanist. To keep the Filipino frightened of the truth, however, Rizal was publicly executed by those in church authority - the ecclesiastical liars gifted with a free will from divinity to promote in the Philippines social insanity. P

SPANISH CATHOLIC FRIARS

In his official biography of Rizal, Guerrero disclosed that the Spanish Catholic friars made a firm offer to Rizal the amount of 100,000 pesos and a chair to teach philosophy at the University of Santo Thomas on the condition that he signed the retraction document. It has been reported by the friars that Rizal did sign his retraction papers. And yet, after Rizal was shot to death at the Luneta by a firing squad, not even a mass in church was said for Rizal who died as a penitent Catholic. In fact, Rizal was not even given a proper Catholic burial. His remains were just thrown in a little corner in Paco cemetery where heretics and infidels were buried.

The trouble with Guerrero as the Rizal biographer, he was more interested in defending the business of the Catholic Church and its teachings than defending truthfully the subject of his biography, Jose Rizal and his teachings.

Rizal never threatened me with eternal hellfire if I did not believe or spread any of his words. In the fight therefore between Rizal and the Catholic Church, I will always be on the side of Rizal. Never will I abandon such a great man even if it means losing my silly soul to end up in a silly hell as managed by a silly devil in cahoots with a silly Supreme Being.

RIZAL'S PREDILECTION

After six months of stay, he left for Europe for the second time on February 3,1888 to pursue the task he had set for himself. His brief stay enabled him to judge the effect of his Noli Me Tangere. He knew he was a marked man for writing the book which not only shook the Spanish rule, but precisely rattled more the foundation of authority in the Philippines - the Catholic church and its teachings.

The military trial of Rizal was not meant to administer justice throughout the land. It was done purposely to execute him in public so that the Filipinos would be frightened to death and subsequently to stop dreaming of freedom under free and humanistic thought. Thus, when the so-called Spanish rule was thrown out with the interference of the US naval forces, what stayed behind to continue controlling Filipino minds and dominating Filipino hearts was the Catholic Church. Via Catholic schools, colleges, and universities, Catholic teachings prevailed in the Philippines . Consider the average Filipino in this 21st century. He is more conversant about the fantastic life and times of Jesus Christ than he knows anything about the realistic life and times of Jose Rizal. And to think Jose Rizal was born in the Philippines - a Christian country. Jesus Christ was born, if at all, in Israel that is today not even a Christian country. It is a Jewish State.

Catholic friars claimed that before he was executed Rizal retracted and asked for the forgiveness of his sin against God and for the pardon of his crime against the Filipino people. These developments, however, are based upon religious hogwash. The Rizal retraction scandal was concocted by the religious cowards. Just as much as the religious cowards of our day, the Knights of Rizal - continue to be afraid to stand up to defend Rizal's great intellectual capacity as a rare Filipino gifted with the capacity not only to think but also to die with self-respect and dignity.

GREAT MEN

France had Voltaire. Germany had Nietzche. Austria had Freud. China had Sun Yet Sen. England had Bertrand Russell. Italy had Galileo and Bruno. America had Tom Paine and Ingersoll. Cuba had Jose Marti and Fidel Castro. These were some of the great men who, with courage and intellect, put more sense into the minds of men and the hearts of women where nature has put only nonsense.

We Filipinos could have had Jose Rizal. The greatest and rarest Filipino this country has ever produced. Unfortunately, the Catholic Church cut him down to size. Millions of Filipinos still have no inkling why Rizal was one of mankind's greatest heroes. Indeed, college professors, historians, biographers, including his own descendants have been frightened by the Catholic Church authority to believe that Rizal was executed while repentant of his sins against God and regretful of his crimes against his own people. What brazen lies to tell about the greatest Filipino thinker who ever lived. The greatest Filipino who died sober and not drunk with sacred lies.

In the meantime, pontifical fear and ecclesiastical ignorance are the recycled garbage dished out in our schools, colleges, and universities. Especially those owned and managed by the Catholic Church and other religious organizations in the Philippines. Consider the average Filipino in this 21st century: he is more comfortable with stupid prayer under a theology than he is at home with intelligent science producing technology to enhance our freedom and democracy.

Indeed, if yesterday Rizal locally was the pride of the

Malay race, today globally he should already be the pride of the human race.

ALBERT EINSTEIN ON JOSE RIZAL

Great spirits have always found opposition from mediocrities. The latter cannot understand it when a man does not thoughtlessly submit to hereditary prejudices but honestly and courageously uses his intelligence and fulfills the duty to express the results of his thoughts in clear form. Indeed, Einstein had in mind men like our own Jose Rizal when he wrote: It keeps repeating itself in this world, so fine and honest: The parson alarms the populace, the genius is executed.

BERTRAND RUSSELL ON JOSE RIZAL

A man who has once perceived, however, temporarily and however briefly, what makes greatness of spirit, can no longer be happy if he allows himself to be petty, self-seeking, troubled by trivial misfortunes, dreading what fate may have in store for him. A man capable of greatness of spirit will open wide the windows of his mind, letting the winds blow freely upon it from every portion of the universe. He will see himself and life and the world as truly as our human limitations will permit; realizing the brevity and minuteness of human life, he will realize also that in individual minds is concentrated whatever of value the known universe contains. And he will see that the man whose mind mirrors the world becomes in a sense as great as the world, In emancipation from the fears that beset the slave of circumstance he will experience a profound joy, and through all the vicissitudes of his outward life he will remain in the depths of being a happy man.

CARL SAGAN ON JOSE RIZAL

As a consequence of the enormous social and technological changes of the last few centuries, the world is not working well. We do not live in traditional and static societies. But our governments, in resisting change, act as if we did. Unless we destroy ourselves utterly, the future belongs to those societies that while not ignoring the reptilian and mammalian parts of our being, enable the characteristically human components of our nature to flourish; to those societies that encourage diversity rather than conformity; to those societies willing to invest resources in a variety of social, political, economic and cultural experiments, and prepared to sacrificed short-term advantage for long-term benefit; to those societies that treat new ideas as delicate, fragile and immensely valuable pathways to the future.

SAM HARRIS ON JOSE RIZAL

We are the final judges of what is good, just as we remain the final judges of what is logical. And on neither front has our conversation with one another reached an end. There need to be no scheme of rewards and punishments transcending this life to justify our moral intuitions or to render them effective in guiding our behavior in the world. The only angels we need to invoke are those of our better nature: reason, honesty, and love. The only demons we must fear are those that lurk inside every human mind: ignorance, hatred, greed, and faith, which is surely the devil\s masterpiece.

RICHARD DAWKINS ON JOSE RIZAL

Fraud, illusion, trickery, hallucination, honest mistake or outright lies, the combination adds up to such a probable alternative that I shall always doubt casual observations or second hand stories that seem to suggest the catastrophic overthrow of existing science. Existing science will undoubtedly be overthrown; not, however, by casual anecdotes or performances on television, (or by public execution of scientists like Rizal) but by rigorous research, repeated, dissected and repeated again.

BUDDHA ON JOSE RIZAL

"Do not believe in anything simply because you have heard it. Do not believe in anything simply because it is spoken and rumored by many.

Do not believe in anything because it is found written in your religious books.

Do not believe in anything merely on the authority of your teachers and elders.

Do not believe in traditions because they have been handed down for many generations. But after observation and analysis, when you find anything that agrees with reason and is conducive to the good and benefit of one and all then accept it and live up to it. Siddharta Buddha

To MY DEAR JOSE RIZAL

Wherever you are, I have the highest respect for you as a man, and I have the deepest love for you as a Filipino. In this connection, I shall continue, to the end of my days, to struggle against those who had you, publicly, put to death. They are still existing, alive and kicking doing more harm, more damage, more evil than ever. Indeed, in this 21st century, your enemies are still in control of our schools, colleges, and universities twisting the mind of the Filipino to remain spiritually poor as a people, and still distorting the heart of the Philippines to remain morally bankrupt as a nation!

Sir: in the God-forsaken country, you are about the one and only Filipino, with dignity and self-respect, worthy to be called Filipino! The rest are trying only to save themselves the trouble of having to think. As the Sick Man of Asia , we only love to believe. Thus, instead of appeals to principles and logic and philosophy, our public spirit is only aroused by personalities and celebrities. Indeed, instead of being the mature masters of our ideals and principles as a society, we only continue to be the childish victims of a foreign Jewish deity. Poch Suzara

RIZAL'S ULTIMO ADIOS

How do we summarize it? The poem was completed on Dec. 29, 1896 hours before he was executed. He was able to smuggle out the finished poem. He placed it inside a lamp and gave to his visitors, among whom was his sister and whispered to her: look inside. There is something inside it. He made an extra copy by putting it inside his shoe for insurance purpose.

The Ultimo Adios was Rizal's last poetic defiance against those who continue to be childish believers instead of being intelligent thinkers. The Ultimo Adios is a strong message to the Filipino as a people: to begin to think that we all share only one common enemy together. No, not the Spaniards or the Americans or the Japanese, or what have you, etc. But our enemy is stupid religion. Indeed, religion that encourages individual stupidity that culminates into social insanity.

MY DREAM

My dream, wrote Rizal to a Spanish governor-general, was my country's prosperity . . . I would like the Filipino people to become worthy, noble, and honorable.

On another occasion Rizal also wrote: I would like the Filipinos to be Brilliant, Enlightened, Intelligent, and Progressive.

Ever since Rizal was executed by the religious morons in the 19th century, the same religious morons carried on with power and authority to be in charge especially of the system of education in the Philippines. Indeed, we were taught in our schools, colleges, and universities to believe and to have faith in the holy bible that clearly states: Love not this world, neither the things that are in the world. If any man love the world, the love of the Father is not with him. John 2:15. Jesus, the loving son of God also preached: If any man come to me and hate not his father, and mother, and wife, and children, and brethren, and sisters, yea, and his own life also, he cannot be my disciple. Luke 14:26

Thus, as the Sick Man of Asia, even the Knights of Rizal continue to ignore what Rizal was saying to all Filipinos more than a century ago. Only people in foreign countries believed, followed, and substantiated what Rizal was saying. After Rizal's execution, the president of the Berlin Society for Anthropology, Ethnology and Pre-history, - Dr. Rudolph Virchow, said: In him we lose not only a true friend of Germany and German science but also the man who had the knowledge and the energy to introduce modern ideas and thinking into the Philippines.

RIZAL WROTE

Where are the youth who will consecrate their golden hours, their dreams, and their enthusiasm to the welfare of their native land? Where are the youth who will generously pour out blood to wash away so much shame, so much crime, so much abomination? Pure and spotless must the victim be! Where are you youth, who will embody in yourselves the vigor of life that has left our veins, the purity of ideas that has been contaminated in our brains, the fire of enthusiasm that has been quenched in our hearts? We await you, O Youth! Come, for we await you!

Ever since the death of Rizal by public execution in 1896, the history of the Filipino people has been the daily, weekly, monthly, and yearly struggle to deny the power of the human mind with knowledge, and to reject the beauty of the human heart with wisdom. Indeed, to be not happy, not sane, and culturally constructive; but only to be unhappy, insane, and traditionally destructive.

Thanks to our teachers in school and professors in our colleges, and universities, millions of Filipinos have yet to learn to substantiate the words of Jose Rizal: I would like the Filipinos to be brilliant, enlightened, intelligent, and progressive.

Sadly, even the Knights of Rizal have been busy promoting social and political insanity in this God-forsaken country. Especially for the sake of preserving in this faith-soaked 21st century the beliefs and values of Christianity.

In this country, when one Pinoy suffers from a delusion, it is called insanity. When millions of Pinoys, however, suffer from a delusion complicated by a confusion, it is called Christianity.

Posted By: Poch SuzaraOn Friday, December 11, 2009

ooo0ooo

10.

Pazogie on Rizal-Pastell's Exchanges And Other Discussions

Pazogie
Dateline, Jan 25, 2017, Postings at
Cepol@yahoogroups.com

Roberto, Check this out about Rizal's biblical and religious knowledge. Are you familiar with Bonoan's dissertation on the Rizal-Pastells Correspondence?

Rizal enrolled in no formal theological courses, but there are numerous indications that he did acquire a more than ordinary layperson's familiarity with Catholic theology. Principal instrument of his theological formation was the religious instruction classes at the Ateneo (Doctrina Cristiana y Moral), but there were other channels. First there were the philosophy courses themselves. Scholastic philosophy was always considered the ancillary handmaid of theology; hence, certain philosophical topics (e.g., person, substance, accident, etc.) necessarily led to classroom discussion on related theological issues. Furthermore, Rizal attended numerous spiritual conferences, sermons, and retreats, which, though probably more devotional in character, inevitably displayed a considerable amount of theological content and form. Then, as an Ateneo alumnus and sodalist, he was invited in 1881 to join the Academia de Ciencias Filosófico-Naturales. The academy was a device set up by the Jesuit Ratio Studiorum (Plan of Studies) designed to foster virtue and stimulate further learning among its members; it was intended principally for sodalists, but membership might also be open to other students, including those enrolled in non-Jesuit institutions. Rizal was elected secretary of the academy and in this capacity kept the actas, or minutes, of the meetings. His records indicate that at the sessions of the academy Father Pablo Ramón, rector of the Ateneo and director of the academy, lectured on strictly theological topics, such as the blessed Trinity and the mystery of revelation.

As a student, Rizal, now become a voracious reader, asked his father to purchase the ten-volume Historia Universal by Césare Cantú, stalwart defender of the rights of the Church, personal friend of Pius IX, and the only layman who attended the First Vatican Council. Cantú, whose explicit, conscious assumption was the providential structure of history as the world moves forward to higher levels of unity and civilization under the leadership of the Church and the papacy, began his work with the creation of the world as described in Genesis, and treated topics of theological import as the nature of religions, the age of the universe, and the Galileo case. No doubt this monumental work stimulated Rizal's interest in theological issues.

Likewise, it was as a student at the Ateneo, that he became familiar with the writings of Don Felix Sardá y Salvany, Catalan diocesan priest, student of the Jesuits and their loyal friend, and a passionate polemicist and prolific publicist known for his crusade against liberalism. His most famous work carried the telling title El liberalismo es pecado and became the manual of the ultra-conservative Integrist Party. Thus Rizal's theological staple in his early years was the writings of men distinguished for their fierce defense of the Church and intense loyalty to the pope.

BobB and CV,

Thanks for reminding me of Bonoan on Rizal-Pastells exchanges. It made me look up my notes and found this "summary" from one blog:

https://marlonborreo.wordpress.com/2007/03/20/jose-rizals-thoughts-on-god/,

prefaced with: condensed from excerpts from Rizal's second, third, and fourth letters to Pastells. A few of the passages cited are direct quotations; most are paraphrased for brevity and clarity. And of course, it wasn't presented like this, enumerated, in the letters.

1. Through reason and by necessity, rather than through faith, do I believe in the existence of a creative Being.

2. Man makes his own God according to his own image and likeness, and then attributes to him his own works.

3. My faith in God is blind, in as much as it know snothing. I neither believe nor disbelieve in the qualities attributed by many to God.

4. I believe in revelation, but not in any of the revelation each religion claim to possess. One cannot but discern the human imprint and the mark of the times in these revelations.

5. Sacred books of religious dogmas are insights of whole generations put down in writing; as such, they are for me God's word.

6. The supernatural light is more perfect than human reason. But there is no one in our small planet who can claim with just reason to be the reflector of this Light.

7. No religion holds supremacy over others.

8. No one can pass judgment on the beliefs of others using his own as the standard.

9. Religions must make men brothers, not enemies of each other. The best religions are those that are simplest.

10. Nature is the only divine book of unquestionable legitimacy. It is the Creator's sole manifestation in this life.

11. I settle for studying God in his creatures like myself.

12. The Creator desires man to perfect himself by growing in knowledge.

13. Everyone must love the neighbor as himself.

14. The soul is immortal. As the atom cannot be annihilated, it is true also for consciousness which rules the atom. Nothing is lost; things merely change.

15. Humanity can fall a thousand times but it will always find salvation.

16. All the subtle arguments to explain the union of God and man in Christ are for me a tour de force of the imagination.

17. No argument can convince me that the Catholic Church is infallible.

18. The heart, the conscience, is God's nobler temple.

19. I am not Protestant.

Many have read Bonoan on these points, like BobB, CV, Poch, MarT, Fred N, MarP, and other Rizalistas. I would just like to refer this list to all those knowledgeable of these letters and of the historical Rizal as a help in making a rational and logical conclusion on Rizal's "faith" at the time he bid us with his final goodbye.

Do you concur with the blogger's understanding as listed, culled simply from the letters? What other documents would contribute in unearthing his "faith"? Letters to Blumentritt, his books, Ultimo Adios, what else?

With all these 19 items considered, what belief system do you think Rizal's "faith" come closest?

If he had lived, what belief system would he have advocated?

With "these 19 items only considered" would you agree that Rizal retracted and returned to the Catholic faith?

I am very eager to hear your answers. Ogie

Roberto Bernardo Posting on
Fr. Raul Bonoan SJ - In the Introduction
Dateline, January 25, 2017 <CePol@yahoogroups.com>

Thanks for this lesson in continuing self-education; it keeps my mind growing even as its bodily housing declines in old age. Pinoys should seriously read Bonoan's book on the Pastells-JPR debate. But they don't but still like to posture in discussions as if they knew enough of the subject. I recall though that Bonoan failed to stress enough a deep truth about our subject: he was a voracious reader-and-disciple of France's most influential Enlightenment writer, thinker, philosopher of science and religion and arch-critic of organized religion. Voltaire! And whom Will Durant considered one of the ten greatest and most influential thinkers of all time.

One of the first things he did in liberal Madrid was buy his complete works in which to self-educate seriously. If we are to understand Rizal fully we should at least read an article about Voltaire. You could say Rizal was the closest PH counterpart of Voltaire himself, and of the Spaniard Pi y Margall.

We should check out too the references in Noli to Zoroastrianism, which he called the much-more ancient father of the three major Abrahamic Religions. This influenced their concepts of heaven and hell, Messiah, future judgment, angels and demons, resurrection, eternal life, etc. As I have kept stressing, with Helen T. most recently, the Pinoy darkeners of Rizal and his Adios, with their powerful promotion of the alleged Retraction and its Complex of Implied Tales, has largely blacked out Pinoy deeper knowledge of Rizal, and why he is the greatest Malayan. Not just according to the pre-war unread Quirino classic, but in the equally unread classic of Austin Coates.

On Wednesday, January 25, 2017 10:57 PM,
"pazogie pazogie2003@yahoo.com
[CePol]"<CePol@yahoogroups.com> wrote:
Thank you for the excerpt on Rizal's religious interest as seen by Bonoan.

My idea of education on Rizal should be done at least in two parts - one for general interest and the other, a deeper and more elaborate for higher learning level - for scholars and other serious interested parties. The general interest may be divided into 3 levels of learning - elementary, intermediate and high school. The deeper more comprehensive part would be a selective subject for college students.

The way we teach Rizal is wrong. For example, the Ultimo Adios is taught to everybody. In my experience , even for high school students this poem is difficult to appreciate.. The interpretation [not translation] of Bob Cottie is proof of the intricacies and ideas that cannot be understood without a good working knowledge of the subject Rizal - of his life and works, his reform advocacy and the world he lived in - local and foreign. The 'trying hard" teacher without doubt would make the 98% percent of the students learn the wrong Ultimo message of Rizal. The emphasis on its beauty would be a misplaced teaching. Some teachers emphasize his genius which 99,9% of the students are not and would certainly not be motivated to emulate Rizal for the simple reason that they are not geniuses. But of course! Many makes the Ultimo the best poem but don't present equally or better ones. Almost everybody would make the students understand that Rizal was a full-fledged doctor of medicine and would not tell or cannot having been made ignorant of the sad experience of the stepfather of Josephine Bracken at the operating table of Rizal, who lost one eye to

Rizal's incompetence and refused to have his other eye operated on for fear that he would become totally blind. He would not let Rizal operate to remove the cataract on the second blurred eye. This patient tried to avenge his loss of sight in one eye by attacking Rizal, intent on beating the shit out of him, but was unsuccessful because 4 kindhearted souls intervened.

On the highest level, scholars should endeavour to propound a Rizal the way he truly was, with practically no ifs or guesses left. He must be sold as a whole and not in unrelated bits and pieces. The whole of the hero must be the emphasis, not his [false or unproven] martyrdom that is clothed with controversy, or his ability as a poet [expecting students to be motivated to become poets?]. Or, his skill to speak 40 languages [for today this is irrelevant; it is sufficient to master only two - English [that is becoming the international language and already made a second language in most countries] and one's native vernacular. If ever there is a need for emphasis it must be on his nationalism because it is on this category where he is generally accepted contributing best [relative to nation building, where lies the most weight on his heroism measure].

For the seniors, I think we can start a monthly SenCit magazine featuring interesting stories of professionals, students or readers of Rizal's books and articles that have helped them succeed [by imbibing the virtues and principles of Rizal; not his faith though that is yet of unknown definition and worth]. Oh, his faith? This will come later, as soon as we have enough success materials to form a scholarly consensus [from embracing the kind of faith Rizal most likely had before he died]

Bye for now,
Ogie

oo0Ooo

11.

Rizal's Apostacy was World Ecumenism
Pazogie
Dateline, January 6, 2017

Bob, personally, I don't think JPR retracted. I cannot forget that you got the goods on that. I don't even think [in deference of an overwhelming opposition, hehe] that he wrote the untitled, undated and unsigned Ultimo Adios, primarily for the reason that there were too much "God-speak" in it, which does not conform [doesn't follow or, not in agreement] with his retraction. Two alleged authoritative jobs contradicting each other by the genius Rizal is totally unthinkable! But not to the Friars who schemed to use them for their evil interest at their own reckoned perfect time for vengeance and deterrence [to douse the growing rebellion], not knowing perhaps that in a future time they will be uncovered. The God-homage in the Poem contradicts and totally extinguishes the integrity of the Retraction. I mean to say, if these two - Retraction and Farewell docs, were premises to the conclusion that JPR died believing once again in the Catholic faith, one premise contradicting the other, the conclusion would not be tenable. The argument becomes unsound. You see, when we push for a no retraction, it means for one important thing, JPR did not go back to Catholicism. If he didn't why would there be, in the Ultimo Adios, too much reference of belief, respect and adoration of a religion and its God he relinquished? Would not this surprising or unexpected homage prod us to critically think into doubt the retraction that may subsequently lead us to believe that he did not write the defective or inconsistent Ultimo Adios? Or, even totally dismiss it as a fraud? For discussion sake, knowing how foxy the Friars were, our creative imagination may fly to a scenario where they concocted an Ultimo Adios to supplement the Retraction [going back to God] because the Retraction alone would not suffice or hold much weight without a supporting corroborative document such as the Ultimo Adios [once again showing homage to God] to achieve their intended purpose of a God believing, once again, Rizal! Let us not forget in our reflections on the matter, the dates of release of the alleged original Poem that came 35 years ahead of the alleged true copy of the Retraction despite the fact that both were announced the day or a few days after Rizal's execution. From the fact of their being simultaneously divulged publicly, would it mean, among other things, from your point of view, that the two complementary docs were needed to be simultaneously known to support the conclusion that Rizal indeed returned to the fold? It's akin to the legal necessity of having two witnesses corroborating each other in order to clinch a claim. It is quite understandable why the sisters of Rizal would claim the Poem to be his if we factor in our analysis the fearful situation of the family Rizal left behind. A dead atheist Rizal certainly would add more serious burdens to the family already made impoverish by the Domicans who during Rizal's active God apostate years secretly vowed vengeance. The family had been dispossessed of their traditional large tract of agricultural land. Won't the family be better off with their Rizal known to have embraced once again the Catholic faith before he was mercilessly shot? Would they not agree to the powerful Friar's preferred contents of the "Love God-Country"Poem in return for a better treatment? Won't the poem help in the propaganda that Rizal retracted to discourage many members of the Katipunan? For me, to deny these possibilities is to deny the bad [evil] genius of the Friars that outwitted the good genius Rizal, twice! First, while campaigning for reforms at the Spanish Parliament and second, during his last month of life. Many Filipinos would not want Rizal to disown the Ultimo Adios. Why? Because it had been nationally and internationally acclaimed a most fitting masterpiece to the total happiness of all Filipinos, here and abroad; a masterpiece, unimaginable then to come from the hitherto unknown unheralded Filipino race of no known great fames! And translated into many languages throughout the whole World, WOW! Filipinos are very proud to receive such a great honor never before bestowed upon any Filipino. Ok, so who is the foolish Filipino who would want to make another, whoever, other than Rizal, own the Poem? No one except crazy Ogie who believes also that Rizal's great stature and heroism would not be diminished, not a bit or an iota, if he didn't write it. Know something else that is crazy? Well, here. The poem makes me doubt his loyalty at the time; made me think he had to be loyal first to Spain, then eventually, at the right time when his islas have been united and became independent, his loyalty will naturally be first for the new Filipino nation, next to Spain; a dual. Hey, who is the genius who will renounce his allegiance to a World Power when there was no Filipino nation YET to speak about? Nakaseguro na si Genius sa Spain, di ba? Tingnan na lang ang tratamento nila sa kanya sa Dapitan at ang pagpayag sa kanyang biyahe sa Cuba at pagbigay sa mga hiniling niya? Bobo siya kung piliin niya, una, sina SURELOSERS Boni at Agui at ang itatayo pa lang na bayang KATAGALOGAN! Galing yata siya sa Dapitan na naging successful capitalist siya at doon nasabi na niya kay Katipunero Dr. Pio V na tatalunin sila. Eh, gago siya na doon poporma sapamamaril o panaksak sa panig ng seguradong talo! Besides, there were at thetime only thousands of separate islands that has not yet been consolidated into one nation! Hindi po ba binobobo natin si Rizal tuwing nagpupumilit tayo na ang loyalty niya ng panahon binaril siya ay sa Filipino Nation? Aba, e, ang puso niya ay nasa Filipino lagi, pero loyalty to a country? [Hindi lang kasi nila narining ang dugtong ng isinisigaw niyang huling mga salita nung barilin siya,na nagsimula VI-VA...ES na ang kasunod sana ay, panya! Ganun din sina Gomburza, na nagsusumigaw, Hindi kami traydor sa Espanya. Hindi totoo ang paratang nila na nagtraydo kami! E, ano ba, hoy gising, ang ibig sabihin nito?; [I am not guilty of the charge of rebellion against me! Read my defense!!! argued Rizal. Does that not say much of his loyalty to Spain? It bothers me. I think soon it may bother you, too.] I can just imagine the smug smile of success on the faces of the evil Friars who masterminded the Poem and Retraction. I believe that the Friars who allegedly witnessed the Retraction and

Wedding were the very ones who authored both the Retraction and Poem. The Wedding may also be thought of as a part of the supporting docs. [TRIVIA: The Friars also authored the fiestas "Cebu Sto Nino Sinulog and possibly the Battle of Mactan." Haay, if Filipinos can only go deeper into the Magellan story with documents in the darkened dusty archives of Spain and Portugal, they might be made to think that Magellan's true purpose were not spices but lands for Spain [particularly those that were being fraudulently claimed by Portugal] and he was killed in a MUTINY led by Juan Sebastian Elcano and that there was no Lapulapu in a settlement in a barren Mactan corral island, a settlement with no vegetation and fresh water rivers for Lapulapu and his people to live on? Naku po naman, ano ba naman iyan! There's the Sto. Nino icon, made of black woodor dyed black [not burnt blackened as claimed and found in a burnt chapel] with Portuguese eyes not sparkling Spanish eyes! Hehe, a sculptress was successful in making one eye look Spanish but she quit when she fell down the steps after the task, leaving the other eye still looking Portuguese. The icon came from the Portuguese [after the Moors] that frequented the islands long before the Spaniards that came later starting with Magellan. But don't worry, my ardent believers of the Friars, the Sinulog and Battle of Mactan fiestas will go on. What about, Magellan being killed by Lapulapu? That too. Unless... oh, Du30... he may hate the Friars, hmm, but the murder of Magellan, a mutiny, boots in tandem, an EJK? Hmm, I don't like to think about it. hehehe...]
Ogie

ooOOoo

12.

When Philosophy Lost Its Way

By ROBERT FRODEMAN
and ADAM BRIGGLE

Dateline, JANUARY 11, 2016

The Stone is a forum for contemporary philosophers and other thinkers on issues both timely and timeless. The Stone is a gathering of opinion around the web.

Students at the University of California at **Berkeley**. Credit Jim Wilson/The New York Times

The history of Western philosophy can be presented in a number of ways. It can be told in terms of periods — ancient, medieval and modern. We can divide it into rival traditions (empiricism versus rationalism, analytic versus Continental), or into various core areas (metaphysics, epistemology, ethics). It can also, of course, be viewed through the critical lens of gender or racial exclusion, as a discipline almost entirely fashioned for and by white European men.

The philosopher's hands were never clean and were never meant to be.

Yet despite the richness and variety of these accounts, all of them pass over a momentous turning point: the locating of philosophy within a modern institution (the research university) in the late 19th century. This institutionalization of philosophy made it into a discipline that could be seriously pursued only in an academic setting. This fact represents one of the enduring failures of contemporary philosophy.

Take this simple detail: Before its migration to the university, philosophy had never had a central home. Philosophers could be found anywhere — serving as diplomats, living off pensions, grinding lenses, as well as within a university. Afterward, if they were "serious" thinkers, the expectation was that philosophers would inhabit the research university. Against the inclinations of Socrates, philosophers became experts like other disciplinary specialists. This occurred even as they taught their students the virtues of Socratic wisdom, which highlights the role of the philosopher as the non-expert, the questioner, the gadfly.

Philosophy, then, as the French thinker Bruno Latour would have it, was "purified" — separated from society in the process of modernization. This purification occurred in response to at least two events. The first was the development of the natural sciences, as a field of study clearly distinct from philosophy, circa 1870, and the appearance of the social sciences in the decade thereafter. Before then, scientists were comfortable thinking of themselves as "natural philosophers" — philosophers who studied nature; and the predecessors of social scientists had thought of themselves as "moral philosophers."

The second event was the placing of philosophy as one more discipline alongside these sciences within the modern research university. A result was that philosophy, previously the queen of the disciplines, was displaced, as the natural and social sciences divided the world between them.

This is not to claim that philosophy had reigned unchallenged before the 19th century. The role of philosophy had shifted across the centuries and in different countries. But philosophy in the sense of a concern about who we are and how we should live had formed the core of the university since the church schools of the 11th century. Before the development of a scientific research culture, conflicts among philosophy, medicine, theology and law consisted of internecine battles rather than clashes across yawning cultural divides. Indeed, these older fields were widely believed to hang together in a grand unity of knowledge — a unity directed toward the goal of the good life. But this unity shattered under the weight of increasing specialization by the turn of the 20th century.

Early 20th-century philosophers thus faced an existential quandary: With the natural and social sciences mapping out the entirety of both theoretical as well as institutional space, what role was there for philosophy? A number of possibilities were available: Philosophers could serve as 1) synthesizers of academic knowledge production; 2) formalists who provided the logical undergirding for research across the academy; 3) translators who brought the insights of the academy to the world at large; 4) disciplinary specialists who focused on distinctively philosophical problems in ethics, epistemology, aesthetics and the like; or 5) as some combination of some or all of these.

If philosophy was going to have a secure place in the academy, it needed its own discrete domain, its own arcane language, its own standards of success and its own specialized concerns.

There might have been room for all of these roles. But in terms of institutional realities, there seems to have been no real choice. Philosophers needed to embrace the structure of the modern research university, which consists of various specialties demarcated from one another. That was the only way to secure the survival of their newly demarcated, newly purified discipline. "Real" or "serious" philosophers had to be identified, trained and credentialed. Disciplinary philosophy became the reigning standard for what would count as *proper* philosophy.

This was the act of purification that gave birth to the concept of philosophy most of us know today. As a result, and to a degree rarely acknowledged, the institutional imperative of the university has come to drive the theoretical agenda. If philosophy was going to have a secure place in the academy, it needed its own discrete domain, its own arcane language, its own standards of success and its own specialized concerns.

Having adopted the same structural form as the sciences, it's no wonder philosophy fell prey to physics envy and feelings of inadequacy. Philosophy adopted the scientific modus operandi of knowledge production, but failed to match the sciences in terms of making progress in describing the world. Much has been made of this inability of philosophy to match the cognitive success of the sciences. But what has passed unnoticed is philosophy's all-too-successful aping of the institutional form of the sciences. We, too, produce research articles. We, too, are judged by the same coin of the realm: peer-reviewed products. We, too, develop sub-specializations far from the comprehension of the person on the street. In all of these ways we are so very "scientific."

Our claim, then, can be put simply: Philosophy should never have been purified. Rather than being seen as a problem, "dirty hands" should have been understood as the native condition of philosophic thought — present everywhere, often interstitial, essentially interdisciplinary and transdisciplinary in nature. Philosophy is a mangle. The philosopher's hands were never clean and were never meant to be.

There is another layer to this story. The act of purification accompanying the creation of the modern research university was not just about differentiating realms of knowledge. It was also about divorcing knowledge from virtue. Though it seems foreign to us now, before purification the philosopher (and natural philosopher) was assumed to be morally superior to other sorts of people. The 18th-century thinker Joseph Priestley wrote "a Philosopher ought to be something greater and better than another man." Philosophy, understood as the love of wisdom, was seen as a vocation, like the priesthood. It required significant moral virtues (foremost among these were integrity and selflessness), and the pursuit of wisdom in turn further inculcated those virtues. The study of philosophy elevated those who pursued it. Knowing and being good were intimately linked. It was widely understood that the point of philosophy was to become good rather than simply to collect or produce knowledge.

NOW IN PRINT
The Stone Reader: Modern Philosophy in 133 Arguments

An anthology of essays from The Times's philosophy series, published by Liveright.

As the historian Steven Shapin has noted, the rise of disciplines in the 19th century changed all this. The implicit democracy of the disciplines ushered in an age of "the moral equivalence of the scientist" to everyone else. The scientist's privileged role was to provide the morally neutral knowledge needed to achieve our goals, whether good or evil. This put an end to any notion that there was something uplifting about knowledge. The purification made it no longer sensible to speak of nature, including human nature, in terms of purposes and functions. By the late 19th century, Kierkegaard and Nietzsche had proved the failure of philosophy to establish any shared standard for choosing one way of life over another. This is how Alasdair MacIntyre explained philosophy's contemporary position of insignificance in society and marginality in the academy. There was a brief window when philosophy could have replaced religion as the glue of society; but the moment passed. People stopped listening as philosophers focused on debates among themselves.

Once knowledge and goodness were divorced, scientists could be regarded as experts, but there are no morals or lessons to be drawn from their work. Science derives its authority from impersonal structures and methods, not the superior character of the scientist. The individual scientist is no different from the average Joe; he or she has, as Shapin has written, "no special authority to pronounce on what ought to be done." For many, science became a paycheck, and the scientist became a "de-moralized" tool enlisted in the service of power, bureaucracy and commerce.

Here, too, philosophy has aped the sciences by fostering a culture that might be called "the genius contest." Philosophic activity devolved into a contest to prove just how clever one can be in creating or destroying arguments. Today, a hyperactive productivist churn of scholarship keeps philosophers chained to their computers. Like the sciences, philosophy has largely become a technical enterprise, the only difference being that we manipulate words rather than genes or chemicals. Lost is the once common-sense notion that philosophers are seeking the good life — that we ought to be (in spite of our failings) model citizens and human beings. Having become specialists, we have lost sight of the whole. The point of philosophy now is to be smart, not good. It has been the heart of our undoing. *(Robert Frodeman and Adam Briggle teach in the department of philosophy and religion and the University of North Texas. They are co-authors of the forthcoming "Socrates Tenured: The Institutions of 21st-Century Philosophy."*

Follow The New York Times Opinion section on Facebook and on Twitter, and sign up for the Opinion Today newsletter.)

ooOOoo

13.

China's Masterstroke

Erick San Juan
Dateline, Jan. 31, 2017

The Manila Times news report quoted Professor Renato de Castro of De La Salle University's international studies department as saying in a forum in Makati City, "Foreign policy has to be democratic. It has to reflect the sentiment of the people."

Just like what the recent survey of Pulse Asia revealed that 8 out of 10 Filipinos or 84 percent want the government to assert Philippine rights over the West Philippine Sea. Another aspect of what the Duterte administration should consider, not just plain independent foreign policy. Yes, independent decision with no foreign influence. But it is another thing when you say it should be influenced by the Filipino people – your constituents. Not just you or the people in your loop.

If an overwhelming 84 percent of Filipinos want the government to uphold our rights to the contested area in the South China Sea/West Philippine Sea, it could mean a more aggressive and firm stand to claim it based on the ruling at The Hague's Permanent Court of Arbitration. So, there seems to be a sort of apprehension on the part of the present leadership in pursuing our rightful claim.

Why is this so?

It should be noted that this is not new when one is dealing with China economically like in other countries. An article by Brahma Chellaney from the Strategist online explains this further – "If there is one thing at which China's leaders truly excel, it is the use of economic tools to advance their country's geostrategic interests.

Through its $1 trillion 'one belt, one road' initiative, China is supporting infrastructure projects in strategically located developing countries, often by extending huge loans to their governments. As a result, countries are becoming ensnared in a debt trap that leaves them vulnerable to China's influence.

Of course, extending loans for infrastructure projects is not inherently bad. But the projects that China is supporting are often intended not to support the local economy, but to facilitate Chinese access to natural resources, or to open the market for low-cost and shoddy Chinese goods. In many cases, China even sends its own construction workers, minimizing the number of local jobs that are created. Remember the shady North Rail project?

Several of the projects that have been completed are now bleeding money. For example, Sri Lanka's Mattala Rajapaksa International Airport, which opened in 2013 near Hambantota, has been dubbed the world's emptiest.

Likewise, Hambantota's Magampura Mahinda Rajapaksa Port remains largely idle, as does the multibillion-dollar Gwadar port in Pakistan. For China, however, these projects are operating exactly as needed: Chinese attack submarines have twice docked at Sri Lankan ports, and two Chinese warships were recently pressed into service for Gwadar port security.

In a sense, it is even better for China that the projects don't do well. After all, the heavier the debt burden on smaller countries, the greater China's own leverage becomes. Already, China has used its clout to push Cambodia, Laos, Myanmar, and Thailand to block a united ASEAN stand against China's aggressive pursuit of its territorial claims in the South China Sea."

And that includes our country as the host of the ASEAN summit where the South China Sea issue is not in the agenda.

"Moreover, some countries, overwhelmed by their debts to China, are being forced to sell to it stakes in Chinese-financed projects or hand over their management to Chinese state-owned firms.

In financially risky countries, China now demands majority ownership up front. For example, China clinched a deal with Nepal this month to build another largely Chinese-owned dam there, with its state-run China Three Gorges Corporation taking a 75% stake."

Another crucial issue that may affect national security matters that we already entered into with China, is our electric power grid. Unfortunately, it is not national as the name of the office implies National Grid Corporation of the Philippines and disguised as not wholly owned by the Philippines but partly owned by the state grid of China.

And still many more agreements with China already in the pipeline as what President Rodrigo Duterte proudly told the Filipino nation. And these are not for free, that is what China termed as soft loan, which they are using soft power to entice nations.

And lastly, why is the biggest (so far) rehabilitation center in the world for drug users is located inside a military camp that is financed and built by China's "philanthropis t". Did we make a due diligence about Rulin who was rumored to be an underworld character in Binondo during the time of Marcos who hastily left for China according to CANU (PC-INP Constabulary Anti-Narcotic Unit of the late Gen. Bienvenido Felix) retired operatives?

Here is what Brahma Chellaney's warning "by integrating its foreign, economic, and security policies, China is advancing its goal of fashioning a hegemonic sphere of trade, communication, transportation, and security links. If states are saddled with onerous levels of debt as a result, their financial woes only aid China's neocolonial designs. Countries that are not yet ensnared in China's debt trap should take note—and take whatever steps they can to avoid it."

I hope that our economic managers who went to China recently were not caught in the trap. Just asking...

oo0Ooo